FRESH & FAST:

MEALS FROM THE MICROWAVE

FRESH & FAST: MEALS FROM THE MICROWAVE

Annette Yates and Norma Miller

RIGHT WAY

Typeset in 9.5 pt Swiss 721 by Letterpart Ltd., Reigate, Surrey.

Printed and bound in Great Britain by Cox & Wyman Ltd., Reading, Berkshire.

The *Right Way* series is published by Elliot Right Way Books, Brighton Road, Lower Kingswood, Tadworth, Surrey, KT20 6TD, U.K. For information about our company and the other books we publish, visit our website at www.right-way.co.uk

Contents

Front cover recipe: Potato and Bacon Salad with Mustard Dressing, page 41.

Photograph by Michael Kay, Solar Studios, Croydon.

Food styling by Taste Talk.

Introduction

Healthy meals and quick meals, fresh and fast – these are the watchwords for modern-day living. The quality of our food is important to us all, but so often we have work, engagements, hobbies and social events pressing upon us, and so little time to spend in our kitchens. So what's to be done?

Make it your mission to get to know your microwave and find out just how versatile it can be. Microwaves have so much to recommend them; they are economical on power by comparison with conventional cooking processes; they are quick, of course, as everyone knows; they are clean to use – no burnt and sticky pans, and much less washing up; and they are much more adaptable when it comes to making food in small quantities.

As food writers running a creative business, with husbands who are equally busy, we value our microwaves for the help they provide, especially for the things that they do particularly well. They are brilliant for sauces, and brilliant for vegetables too, with their concentrated colours and intense flavours, and perfect for puddings, like sponges and cheesecake. Surprising too – such diverse delights as cakes and crunchy toppings, poppadoms and preserves, even sophisticated dining on a small scale, are well within the scope of your microwave's capabilities. And for all day and every day, there is breakfast and brunch, snacks, soups and salads, family favourites and more besides – nourishing and healthy meals, quick and easy to prepare.

Our foolproof and fully-tested recipes use a mixture of fresh and store-cupboard ingredients, readily available from good food stores. There are plenty of serving suggestions and hints and tips to accompany the recipes and make life easier. And whether you are cooking for yourself, for your family or for friends, there are recipes here for every occasion.

So enjoy your voyage of discovery by finding out how your quick, clean, energy-saving microwave can work to your advantage – freshly cooked meals, snacks and extras, puddings, cakes and preserves in all their wonderful variety.

A Helping Hand

This section is all about how to get the best from your microwave and from the recipes in this book. The most important thing to remember is that all the recipes in this book can be cooked in any microwave, no matter what make or model, whether it is a straight microwave or a combination oven. The recipes require no grill or conventional oven heat, just microwaves.

Microwave oven wattage
Every recipe has been tested in microwave ovens with a wattage of 700–800W.

If *your* microwave has a lower wattage (say 500–650W), you may need to cook for a little longer – try out one or two recipes and you will soon get the feel of how our recipes perform in your oven.

If *your* microwave has a higher wattage (say 850–1000W), best results are to be had by simply lowering the power level slightly and cooking for the time given in the recipe.

Microwave power levels
The chart below shows the power levels used to cook the recipes in this book. The higher the wattage, the faster the food cooks, Check your manufacturer's instructions to find the equivalent settings on your microwave oven and make a note of them in the empty column.

High	100%	700–800W	
Medium-High	70–80%	500–600W	
Medium	50%	350–400W	
Medium-Low	30%	200–300W	

Do remember that fast is not always best, especially when cooking small quantities. Should you find that foods are cooking too quickly, drying up around the edges, shrinking, or showing any other signs of overcooking, it may be advisable to cook on a slightly lower power. The extra time taken will be hardly noticeable and the results will be worth it.

Cooking equipment
For the recipes in this book, we have made use of everyday cooking containers that are suitable for microwave cooking: ovenproof casseroles, bowls, shallow dishes and cake dishes, as well as heatproof jugs (but nothing that is chipped or cracked). Where appropriate, we have suggested the shape and size of container in order to produce the best results. Many recipes are cooked in the dishes in which they are served, thus saving on washing up.

When there is any likelihood of the contents boiling up or rising during cooking (soups, sauces, preserves, puddings, cakes), remember to use a large, roomy container.

Instructions for covering (or not) are given in the method of each recipe. When covering a container, use a lid (one to match the container), a large inverted plate or clear film.

Worth a mention
If you are new to microwaving, remember it is fast, very fast.

In ovens without turntables, food may need turning or repositioning occasionally during cooking.

Always follow the manufacturer's instructions when using your microwave oven.

A clean microwave oven is an efficient one. Splashes and spills will attract the microwave energy in their direction instead of it concentrating in the food you want to cook.

Always have oven gloves handy to lift dishes out of the microwave. The oven walls do not get hot but the cooking container will.

The recipes
For convenience, the ingredients are listed in the order in which they are used. Though they are given in imperial as well as metric, in general the metric weights and measures are easier to use. Use one set only.

All spoon measures are level unless otherwise stated.

The recipes include basic store-cupboard ingredients, including the occasional stock cube, liquid stock and, our favourite, vegetable bouillon powder. Because it's granular, you can spoon out as little or as much as you like.

One or two recipes may contain raw or partly cooked eggs – please remember that it is advisable to avoid eating these if you are pregnant, elderly, very young or sick. And while we are on the subject of eggs, do remember that microwave-cooking an egg in its shell is never advisable – it could burst open quite violently and cause damage to your oven or to you!

A few recipes contain fresh chillies. Do take care when preparing them and remember to wash your hands thoroughly afterwards. Better still, wear rubber gloves while handling them.

Salt is kept to a minimum. Instead, we prefer to source good quality ingredients that have bags of flavour. Often, just a handful of freshly chopped herbs, added last minute, is all that may be needed for an extra burst of flavour.

Most of the recipes are so speedy, and they use the minimum amount of liquid, that foods retain their maximum flavour and nutritive value. Vegetables and fruit keep their *fresh colours* – cabbage really is green, carrots are vibrant orange and cherries stay red.

Our recipes tend to use only small amounts of fat, though the quantity can always be adjusted to suit your personal taste.

Very little extra equipment is required to complete the recipes, though we are fond of using a hand-held stick blender for making smooth purées (alternatively, a food processor comes in useful).

Cooking times are always approximate. Microwave ovens differ in their performance from model to model. Ingredients vary in their quality, shape, size and temperature (room temperature or fridge-cold), and so on.

Where it is necessary to heat 150ml/¼ pint water or more (in soups, for instance), we have used the kettle and then added the boiling water to the recipe. This not only saves time but can save energy too.

Please don't simply rely on cooking times. Always use conventional methods of checking that food is cooked – is it tender, soft, cooked through, thickened, bubbling, piping hot; do the juices of meat and poultry run clear; can the fish be separated into flakes; are the vegetables tender; and are the cakes cooked in the centre?

When a recipe needs stirring, covering or a standing time, instructions are given.

Doubling the quantities for a recipe does not lead to doubling the cooking times. Instead, the cooking times should be increased by about 50 per cent. Similarly, if you halve the quantities for a recipe, do not halve the cooking time – reduce it by about one third.

Breakfast & Brunch

1

Early or late morning, busy or relaxed, whatever your situation, you can find yourself wanting to get breakfast or brunch prepared in a hurry, before you turn your mind to more pressing or more inviting things.

With your microwave, hasty food doesn't have to be basic food. In fact, you can have a slap-up breakfast or brunch in just a few minutes. You can warm breads, croissants and pastries gently on low power, and you can make porridge in no time at all – try serving it with some dried fruit softened in the microwave (see page 13). You can do almost anything with eggs in a microwave other than boil them (because the shells will burst open); there are recipes for egg dishes on pages 15–17. And there are special breakfast treats here as well, like kedgeree (on page 18).

So whether you're rushing about or taking it easy, you can be sure to have something hot and delicious from the microwave on the table in little more than the time it takes to boil a kettle.

Sunshine Porridge

A perky start to the day with a simple recipe which seems to have almost endless variations. You don't even need to have weighing scales; use a cup, or mug if you prefer a larger portion, to measure the oats and use the same cup or mug to measure the water. You can replace half of the oats with rye or oat flakes. Make it with water, milk, milk plus unsweetened fruit juice, or milk alternatives made from soya or rice. Depending on your mood or the season, stir into the cooked porridge a spoonful of natural yogurt and/or a handful of blueberries, strawberries, raspberries or grapes. Add a sliced apple, small banana, stoned apricot or plums; a few pieces of one or two ready-to-eat dried fruits – cranberries, prunes, figs, jumbo raisins or apricots; a few chopped shelled nuts such as almonds, walnuts or toasted hazelnuts; or a spoonful of seeds – pumpkin, linseed or sunflower. The porridge will have natural sweetness from the fresh or dried fruits. If you're not feeling so virtuous, sweeten with a little clear honey, maple syrup or soft brown sugar. On celebration days treat yourself by adding a spoonful of cream.

Serves 1

½ cup jumbo oats

1. Put the oats into a large bowl and pour over one cup of cold water.

2. Cook (no need to cover) on Medium-High for 4–5 minutes, stirring once or twice, until the porridge thickens and boils.

3. Stir in a handful of your favourite fruit, nuts or seeds (see above). Leave to stand for a minute before eating.

Fruit Compôte

Use your microwave as a quick way to plump up dried fruits. We've used dried cranberries rather than fresh or frozen as they have a sweeter taste. Serve warm or cold with hot pancakes, also delicious with ice cream. Eat at any time of the day.

Serves 4

8 ready-to-eat dried apricots
8 dried apple rings
6 ready-to-eat dried figs
300ml/½ pint unsweetened black grape juice
2 tbsp clear honey
1 cinnamon stick
2 star anise
55g/2 oz dried cranberries
55g/2 oz golden sultanas

1. Cut the apricots and apple rings in half, and the figs into quarters.

1. Pour the grape juice into a medium casserole and stir in the honey, cinnamon stick and star anise. Cover and cook on High for 3 minutes.

2. Stir in the apricots, apple rings, figs, cranberries and sultanas. Cover and cook on Medium for about 12 minutes, stirring twice, until the fruits have softened.

3. Leave to stand for 30 minutes before serving to allow the flavours to develop.

Traditional Breakfast for One

A great way to treat yourself or a special guest. There's no added fat, unless of course you prefer to add some, in which case, put a small piece of butter or a teaspoonful of oil with the bacon in step 2. Alternatively, try drizzling a little olive oil, chef-like, over the cooked breakfast just before serving.

Serves 1

3–4 mushrooms, about 70g/2½ oz in total
1 medium tomato
2 back bacon rashers
1 egg
A few chopped chives (optional)
Freshly milled salt and pepper (optional)

1. Cut the mushrooms and tomato into quarters.

2. With scissors, cut the bacon rashers into strips about 2.5cm/1 inch wide and scatter them in a shallow ovenproof dish measuring about 15cm/6 inches in diameter. Cook (no need to cover) on High for 1–1½ minutes or until the bacon just begins to brown on the edges.

3. Stir in the mushrooms and cook (no need to cover) on High for 1 minute.

4. Push the bacon mixture in a ring-shape to the sides of the dish and arrange the tomato quarters on top. Break the egg into the centre of the dish and, with the point of a knife, prick the yolk in two places.

5. Cook (still no need to cover) on High for about 2 minutes until the tomatoes have softened slightly and the egg is just set.

6. Serve immediately, sprinkled with a few chopped chives if wished and seasoned to taste.

Bacon, Mushroom and Tomato Open Omelette

The cooking time is for fridge-cold eggs. Eggs at room temperature are likely to cook more quickly. Serve hot or cold. It makes a delicious filling for crusty rolls.

Serves 2

2 smoked bacon rashers
3 or 4 chestnut mushrooms
6 cherry tomatoes
4 medium eggs
Freshly milled salt and pepper
A little chopped fresh parsley or basil (optional)
2 tsp oil

1. With scissors, cut the rind from the bacon rashers then cut the bacon into small pieces. Thickly slice the mushrooms. Halve the tomatoes. Lightly beat the eggs with a little seasoning, stirring in a little chopped parsley or basil (if using).

2. Put the oil into a 20cm/8 inch shallow flan dish or cake dish and stir in the bacon. Cook (no need to cover) on High for 1 minute.

3. Stir in the mushroom slices and tomato halves and spread them evenly over the dish. Cook (no need to cover) on High for 1½ minutes.

4. Pour the beaten eggs over the bacon mixture, tilting the dish to spread it evenly. Cook (no need to cover) on Medium for 5–6 minutes, moving the cooked egg from the edges to the centre of the dish once or twice, until almost set.

5. Leave to stand for 3 minutes (it will continue to set) before cutting into wedges and serving.

Scrambled Eggs

The secret to scrambling eggs in the microwave is to stay with them and watch them, checking and stirring frequently – just as you would when cooking on the hob. We have used medium eggs straight from the fridge – eggs at room temperature will probably cook more quickly. If the eggs cook too fast on High, reduce the microwave power to Medium – it's worth the extra seconds to get a softer, creamier result.

Serves 2

15–25g/½–1 oz butter
5 medium eggs
Freshly milled salt and pepper

1.   Cut the butter into small pieces. Break the eggs into a bowl, add a little salt and pepper. Using a fork, beat the eggs just until the yolks and whites are well mixed. Add the butter.
2.   Cook the eggs uncovered on High, stirring every 30 seconds to mix the cooked parts around the edge with the runny egg mixture in the centre. This should take about 2–2½ minutes.
3.   When the eggs reach a stage when they are not quite as set as you would like, let them stand for a minute to finish cooking. (Use this time to heat up some bread rolls, bagels or croissants on Medium-Low.)

Serving Suggestions
Spoon the hot eggs:
● onto thick slices of wholemeal toast, onto split warmed or toasted bagels, or into warmed and split croissants.

Variations
Into the egg at the end of step 1, stir:
● a spoonful of wholegrain mustard
● chopped roasted red pepper (from a jar)
● chopped capers (washed and dried first)
● thinly sliced spring onions or chopped red onion
● a spoonful of pesto (basil sauce)
● chopped fresh herbs – chervil, tarragon or parsley
● a splash of chilli sauce
● a few black or green olives, stoned and chopped
● a few cooked and chopped asparagus spears.

Baked Eggs on Creamy Spinach

Whole eggs tend to cook more evenly from room temperature rather than fridge-cold. It's important to pierce the yolks in a couple of places and, if they still 'spit', reduce the microwave power to Medium in order to cook them more slowly. We don't bother to cover the eggs during cooking but you may get even better results by topping the dishes with pierced clear film. Remember, when doubling the quantities you will need to increase the cooking times below by about 50 per cent.

Serves 1–2

150g/5½ oz baby spinach leaves
2 tbsp double cream
Generous pinch of freshly grated nutmeg
Freshly milled salt and black pepper
2 small pieces of butter, plus extra for greasing
2 medium eggs

1. Put the spinach into a bowl or casserole, cover and cook on High for 3 minutes.

2. Tip the hot spinach into a sieve and chop it roughly (this is easy to do with kitchen scissors). With the back of a spoon, press out as much liquid as possible – you should be left with 2–3 tbsp spinach. Tip the spinach back into the bowl/casserole and stir in the cream, nutmeg and seasoning.

3. Lightly butter two small (ramekin) dishes, about 7cm/2¾ inches in diameter and 4cm/1½ inches deep. Divide the spinach mixture between the dishes, levelling the surface. Crack an egg into each and, with the pointed tip of a sharp knife, pierce each yolk in two places. Place a piece of butter on top of each egg.

4. Cook on Medium-High for 2–2½ minutes, turning the dishes half way through, or until the eggs are very nearly cooked to your liking. Let them stand for about 30 seconds before serving.

Kedgeree

Our version of this classic brunch dish, a mixture of ready-cooked rice and smoked fish. You could substitute cooked smoked chicken for the fish. Serve with lots of hot toasted brown bread.

Serves 4

1 red onion
1 small lemon
6 cherry tomatoes
6 button mushrooms
Small bunch of fresh flat-leaved parsley
Small bunch of fresh chives
200g/7 oz smoked mackerel or salmon
2 tsp olive oil
2 tsp chicken bouillon powder
250g/9 oz cooked long-grain rice
2 tbsp peas, fresh or frozen
1 tbsp capers
1 tsp paprika pepper

1. Put the kettle on to boil. Thinly slice the onion. Grate the rind from half the lemon, cut in half, squeeze the juice from the grated half and cut the other half into four slices. Quarter the cherry tomatoes and the mushrooms. Finely chop the parsley and chives. Flake the mackerel or cut the salmon into strips.

2. Spoon the oil into a casserole and stir in the onion. Cover and cook on High for 3 minutes until softened.

3. Stir in the bouillon powder, 150ml/¼ pint boiling water (from the kettle), the tomatoes and mushrooms. Cover and cook on High for 1 minute.

4. Stir in the lemon rind and juice, fish, rice, peas, capers and paprika pepper. Cover and cook on High for 6 minutes until piping hot, stirring once.

5. Stir in the chopped parsley and chives, spoon onto hot plates and top with the lemon slices.

Pancetta and Chestnut Mushrooms with Crushed Fennel Potatoes

A smart dish for brunch, light lunch or supper. Pancetta is Italian cured, unsmoked bacon. Sliced breakfast sausage, diced gammon or seafood would make excellent alternatives.

Serves 4

1 medium red onion
1 garlic clove
400g/14 oz red-skinned potatoes
150g/5½ oz pancetta
175g/6 oz chestnut mushrooms
1 small head of Chinese leaves
Handful of parsley sprigs
2 tsp olive oil
½ tsp fennel seeds
2 tbsp wholegrain mustard
1 tbsp brown sauce
2 tbsp milk
Freshly milled salt and black pepper

1. Put the kettle on to boil. Chop the onion and garlic. Roughly dice the potatoes and the pancetta. Thinly slice the mushrooms and shred the Chinese leaves. Finely chop the parsley.

2. Put the oil, onion, garlic and pancetta into a medium casserole, cover and cook on High for 2 minutes, stirring half-way through.

3. Stir in the fennel seeds, mustard, brown sauce, milk and a little seasoning. Cover and cook on High for 1 minute.

4. Mix in the potatoes and mushrooms, cover and cook on High for 6 minutes, stirring once or twice.

5. Stir in the shredded Chinese leaves and the chopped parsley. Cover and cook on High for about 2 minutes until the potatoes are cooked.

6. Use a potato masher or a fork to crush the potatoes a little, stir and serve immediately.

Snappy Snacks

We all like to snack; it's the modern way of life. But so many ready-made snacks come with a health warning: too much fat, too much sugar, too many additives, too much salt.

To avoid these pitfalls, here are some whizzy ideas for snappy snacks – quick and easy to make, healthy and nutritious, tasty and satisfying. They make ideal light bites for busy people who are always in a hurry with no time to lose. So stop a moment, and try something on toast or a hot sandwich, maybe for yourself or to share with someone else.

Economical and customised for convenience, these lip-smacking snacks will have universal appeal. Just contemplate the recipes for halloumi cheese with wholegrain mustard and pesto topping (on page 23), Smart Hot Dogs (on page 28), and corn on the cob with a sticky chilli glaze (on page 21). Fresh food on the run, and so much fun.

Hot Buttery Chilli Corn-on-the-Cob

Crunchy, spicy corn-on-the cob is always popular. Push a short wooden skewer in each end of the cooked corn for ease of handling.

Serves 2

2 cobs of sweetcorn
1 shallot
1 garlic clove
1 red chilli (see page 10)
25g/1 oz butter
1 tbsp brown sugar
Freshly milled salt and black pepper

1. Cut each cob of sweetcorn into three. Finely chop the shallot and garlic. Halve the chilli, remove and discard the seeds and slice thinly.

2. Put the butter into a small bowl and mix in the shallot, garlic, chilli, sugar and a little seasoning.

3. Arrange the pieces of corn in a casserole and spread a little flavoured butter on top of each one.

4. Cover and cook on High for 6 minutes, rearranging them once or twice during cooking, until piping hot and tender. Spoon over any excess sauce and serve warm.

Spiced Chickpeas

A bowl of piping hot chickpeas is just the thing when you are feeing peckish. Very filling and tasty, it will certainly keep you going.

Serves 2

1 small onion
2 garlic cloves
3 large tomatoes
Small bunch of parsley
55g/2 oz Parmesan cheese
400g can chickpeas
2 tsp olive oil
1 tsp chilli paste
2 tbsp tomato purée
1 tbsp vegetable bouillon powder
Freshly milled salt and black pepper
Warm crusty bread, to serve

1. Put the kettle on to boil. Finely chop the onion and crush the garlic. Roughly chop the tomatoes and finely chop the parsley. Coarsely grate the cheese and drain the chickpeas.

2. Put the onion, garlic and oil into a casserole. Cover and cook on High for 3 minutes until softened.

3. Stir in the chickpeas, chopped tomatoes, chilli paste, tomato purée, bouillon powder and 150ml/¼ pint boiling water (from the kettle). Cover and cook on Medium-High for about 8 minutes, stirring twice, until piping hot.

4. Season if necessary and scatter over the chopped parsley and grated cheese.

5. Serve with warm crusty bread.

Halloumi Mushroom Burger

Burger with a difference – filled with a whole flat-cap mushroom and halloumi topped with wholegrain mustard and pesto – no need for pickles. Halloumi is a Cypriot cheese and perfect for cooking.

Serves 1

2 spring onions
1 flat-cap mushroom
2 tsp wholegrain mustard
2 tsp pesto
2 slices of halloumi cheese
1 tsp oil
1 wholemeal bun
Salad leaves

1. Finely chop the spring onions. Trim the mushroom stalk (if any) level with the mushroom cap.

2. In a small bowl mix together the mustard and pesto and stir in the spring onions. Spread some of the mixture over each halloumi slice.

3. Brush both sides of the mushroom with the oil and put into a shallow dish. Cover and cook on High for 3 minutes.

4. Turn the mushroom over and with a slice lift the topped halloumi into the casserole. Cover and cook on High for 3 minutes until the cheese is hot.

5. Cut open the wholemeal bun and add a handful of salad leaves. Add the mushroom and top with the halloumi slices. Replace the lid and serve immediately.

Mushrooms in Garlic and Cheese Sauce

Serve this creamy mixture on thick toasted bread such as French bread or Italian-style ciabatta, or just with fresh crusty bread. We have used chestnut mushrooms for their meaty texture and flavour but you could make it even more special by using a mixture of wild mushrooms – simply tear them into pieces.

Serves 2

400g/14 oz chestnut mushrooms
4 spring onions
100g packet soft cheese with garlic and parsley, such as
**   French roulé**
1 tbsp dry white vermouth, white wine or dry sherry
Freshly milled salt and black pepper

1. Cut the mushrooms into thick slices. Trim the spring onions and slice them thinly, keeping the white and green parts separate.

2. In a small bowl, blend together the cheese and vermouth. Stir in the white onion slices.

3. Put the mushrooms into a casserole, cover and cook on High for 5 minutes, stirring once, until they begin to soften and there is a small amount of mushroom juice in the casserole.

4. Stir in the cheese mixture until the mushrooms are well coated. Cover and cook on High for about 3 minutes, stirring once, until the sauce is creamy and the mushrooms are piping hot throughout.

5. Season to taste and serve with the green onion slices scattered on top.

Mozzarella and Feta Cheese Spread

This rich mixture can be served warm or cold. It goes particularly well with toasted pitta bread and a few black olives. When cold it makes an ideal sandwich filling with some crisp lettuce leaves and thin slices of tomato.

Serves 4

100g/3½ oz mozzarella cheese
100g/3½ oz feta cheese
1 large egg
4 tbsp double cream
1 tbsp chopped fresh herbs, such as mint or chives
Freshly milled black pepper
Crusty bread, toast or crisp biscuits, to serve

1. Cut the cheeses into small cubes. Add the egg, cream, herbs and black pepper and beat well until smooth.

2. Spoon the mixture into four small (ramekin) dishes, about 7cm/2¾ inches in diameter and 4cm/1½ inches deep, and level the surface.

3. Cook (no need to cover) on Medium-High for about 8 minutes, turning or rearranging the dishes once, until the mixture is softly set and piping hot throughout.

4. Leave to stand for 5 minutes before serving. Spoon the cheese spread straight from the dish onto crusty bread, toast or crisp biscuits.

Melted Swiss Cheese Dip with Crusty Bread

A Swiss cheese fondue is transformed from an occasional 'après-ski' treat to a quick-and-easy, warming snack that is fun to share with a friend. Gruyère and Emmenthal cheeses combine to give a traditional flavour and stringiness. Sometimes we add a small pinch each of freshly grated nutmeg and ground white pepper, and a teaspoon or two of kirsch.

Serves 2

1 small garlic clove
100g/3½ oz Gruyère cheese
100g/3½ oz Emmenthal cheese
½ tsp cornflour
100ml/3½ fl oz dry white wine or cider
1 tsp lemon juice
Small chunks of crusty bread, for dipping

1. Halve the garlic clove and, with the cut surfaces, rub the inside of a medium bowl. Discard the garlic.

2. Grate the cheeses and combine with the cornflour.

3. Pour the wine (or cider) and lemon juice into the garlic-rubbed bowl. Cook on High (no need to cover) for about 1 minute or until the liquid just comes to the boil.

4. Stir the cheese mixture into the hot liquid and cook on Medium for about 4 minutes, stirring occasionally, until well mixed, melted and smooth.

5. Serve immediately with chunks of crusty bread for dipping.

Prawns and Vegetables with Black Bean Sauce

A taste of the Orient. Serve in bowls with crusty bread or, for a more substantial meal, with hot rice or noodles.

Serves 2

2 spring onions
4 canned water chestnuts
1 carrot
1 courgette
6 baby sweetcorn
6 button mushrooms
1 tbsp olive oil
1 tbsp lime juice
100g/3½ oz sugar-snap peas
200g/7 oz shelled, raw prawns
2 tbsp black bean sauce
2 tsp light soy sauce
2 handfuls of spinach leaves

1. Thinly slice the spring onions and water chestnuts. Cut the carrot and courgette into thin strips. Thickly slice the baby sweetcorn and quarter the mushrooms.

2. Put the carrot, courgette and sweetcorn into a casserole and stir in the oil, lime juice and 2 tbsp water. Cover and cook on High for 5 minutes.

3. Stir in the sliced spring onions, mushrooms, sugar-snap peas, water chestnuts, prawns, black bean sauce and soy sauce. Cover and cook on High for 4 minutes, stirring twice, until piping hot.

4. Stir in the spinach leaves; they will begin to wilt in the heat. Serve immediately.

Smart Hot Dogs

Yes, hot dogs can be smart if you use fresh crusty bread and good-quality frankfurters, cheese and mustard. We find it difficult to resist adding a dollop of tomato ketchup too. If time allows, why not brown some thinly sliced onions first, as described on page 103.

Serves 2

2 pieces of crusty baguette, each about 15cm/6 inches long
2 tsp mustard, such as Dijon, or to taste
140g packet frankfurters (4)
2 slices of cheese, each weighing about 25g/1 oz, such as Jarlsberg

1. Split a piece of bread along its length, leaving one side intact to make a 'hinge'. Spread half the mustard over the cut surface and fill with two frankfurters and one slice of cheese (you may need to fold it to make an even layer that will sit inside the bread). Fold the top of the baguette over the filling and secure it by pushing a wooden cocktail stick from top to base. Repeat with the remaining bread, mustard, frankfurters and cheese.

2. Place the filled bread on a double layer of kitchen paper and put into the microwave. Heat on High until the bread and frankfurters are warm and the cheese has softened – one should take about 50–60 seconds, two should take 1¼–1¾ minutes.

Hot Barbecue-style Chicken Sandwich

This is delicious served in a fresh crusty baguette with some crisp salad leaves and maybe a little chopped spring onion.

Serves 1

1 tbsp chutney, such as tomato or apple and walnut
1 tbsp tomato ketchup
1 tsp wholegrain mustard
1 tsp olive oil
1 skinless, boneless chicken breast
Crusty roll or baguette of your choice

1. In a bowl, stir together the chutney, tomato ketchup, mustard and oil.

2. Cut the chicken into thin strips and add them to the bowl, stirring to coat them with the mixture.

3. Cook (no need to cover) on Medium-High for 3–4 minutes, stirring twice, or until cooked through.

4. Leave to stand for 1–2 minutes.

5. Split the roll or baguette and fill with the hot chicken and its sauce. Serve immediately.

Speedy Soups

3

Soups come in all sizes, from soup in a cup or a bowl for one or two, or as a starter or appetiser for maybe three or four people, right up to a hearty, substantial main meal for friends. All you need in addition is some good crusty bread to go with it.

Quick and easy to make, soups are always comforting and nourishing, and a great stimulus to the appetite. Be sure to use a large, deep container to allow plenty of room for the contents to boil up. A hand-held stick-blender comes in handy to make the soup as smooth or as chunky as you like. Leftovers can easily be reheated, and you can always make a flavourful stock (see the guidance for making chicken and fish stocks opposite).

With your microwave and a few straightforward, fresh ingredients ready to hand, you can, whenever you like, work a little magic and conjure up some superb soup, a healthy and revitalising treat in just a matter of minutes.

Home-made Stock

Why not use your microwave to make small quantities of home-made stock.

Vegetable
Use a mixture of chopped vegetables (no need to peel them, just wash well) such as onions, leeks, garlic, carrots, celery, celeriac, parsnips, cabbage, tomatoes and red or yellow peppers. Vegetable peelings can be used too (including mushrooms, celery tops and tomato skins) as well as fresh herbs.

Fish
Use bones, heads and trimmings from white fish – plaice, cod, haddock, hake, sole, turbot and whiting – and shellfish, such as prawns. Add a small onion and a carrot, both chopped, and a splash of dry white wine.

Poultry
Raw bones are likely to give the best flavour though a cooked carcass produces good stock too (break it up into small pieces. Add a whole onion, with its skin on, and it will give the stock a lovely golden colour.

Basic method:

1.   Put the vegetables, fish trimmings or poultry bones into a large casserole with a few whole black peppercorns, a small lemon (roughly chopped) and some fresh herbs – sprigs of thyme and parsley, and a bay leaf. Pour over sufficient cold water to cover.
2.   Cook on High until the mixture comes to the boil, then reduce the microwave power to Medium-Low and cook for 30 minutes (vegetable), 15 minutes (fish) or 45 minutes (poultry). Use a slotted spoon to remove any surface scum occasionally during cooking.
3.   Strain through a fine sieve or a colander lined with muslin (before lining the colander, wet the muslin and wring out excess water).
4.   If you plan to use the stock as it is, check the seasoning, adding salt and pepper to taste. For a more concentrated flavour reduce the stock by returning the liquid to the casserole and cooking (do not cover) on High until the stock has reduced by about half. Season lightly with salt and pepper if wished.
5.   Use immediately, or cool and refrigerate for up to 2 days, or freeze.

Tomato, Carrot and Courgette Soup

Bottles or cartons of passata are such useful store-cupboard ingredients, perfect to use when making quick soups and sauces.

Serves 2

1 medium red onion
2 garlic cloves
1 small red pepper
1 large carrot
1 large courgette
1 slice of focaccia bread
4 black olives, stoned
2 tsp olive oil
2 sprigs of fresh oregano
300ml/½ pint passata or sieved tomatoes
1 tsp red wine vinegar
2 tsp vegetable bouillon powder
Freshly milled salt and black pepper

1. Put the kettle on to boil. Finely chop the onion and garlic. Cut the pepper in half, remove and discard the seeds and stalk, and slice thinly. Coarsely grate the carrot and courgette. Tear the bread into small pieces and roughly chop the olives.

2. Put the onion, garlic, carrot and oil into a large casserole. Cover and cook on High for about 3 minutes until softened.

3. Stir in the red pepper, courgette, oregano, passata, red wine vinegar, bouillon powder and 300ml/½ pint boiling water (from the kettle). Cover and cook on High for about 4 minutes until the vegetables are soft.

4. Stir in the pieces of focaccia bread and the olives then season if necessary and serve immediately. If you prefer a smooth soup, whizz with a stick-blender and reheat.

Red Lentil Soup with Rice and Lemon

A chunk of crusty bread is all that is needed to accompany this soup.

Serves 2

1 large onion
1 tbsp olive oil
1 tsp ground coriander
1 tsp ground cumin
1 chicken stock cube or 2 tsp vegetable bouillon powder
100g/3½ oz red lentils
50g/1¾ oz pudding rice or risotto rice
Freshly milled salt and black pepper
Lemon wedges, to serve

1. Put the kettle on to boil. Thinly slice the onion and put into a large casserole with the oil. Cover and cook on High for about 5 minutes until very soft.

2. Stir the coriander and cumin into the onion and add the stock cube or powder. Pour over 1 litre/1¾ pints boiling water (from the kettle) and add the lentils and rice.

3. Cook (no need to cover) on Medium for 15–20 minutes until the lentils and rice are very soft.

4. Season to taste and, if the soup is too thick, thin with a little extra boiling water (from the kettle).

5. Accompany each serving with a lemon wedge for squeezing over.

Mushroom, Celeriac and Walnut Soup

Celeriac is a knobbly root vegetable with a distinct flavour that is similar to celery. It tends to discolour when cut, so use it immediately or put it in a bowl of cold water with a little lemon juice until you need it. Serve this tasty soup with lots of hot crusty bread.

Serves 2

2 shallots
1 garlic clove
175g/6 oz celeriac
175g/6 oz button mushrooms
Small bunch of fennel
6 walnut halves
1 tbsp lemon juice
1 tsp chilli paste
2 tsp vegetable bouillon powder
2 tbsp crème fraîche
Freshly milled black pepper
Hot crusty bread, to serve

1. Put the kettle on to boil. Finely chop the shallots and crush the garlic. Coarsely grate the celeriac or cut it into very fine shreds. Thinly slice the mushrooms. Finely chop the fennel and break the walnut halves into small pieces.

2. Put the shallots, garlic, celeriac, lemon juice, chilli paste and bouillon powder into a large casserole. Pour over 600ml/1 pint boiling water (from the kettle). Stir well, cover and cook on High for 5 minutes until the vegetables are soft.

3. Stir in the mushrooms, walnuts and fennel. Cover and cook on High for 3 minutes.

4. Stir in the crème fraîche, season with a little black pepper and serve immediately with hot crusty bread.

Onion, Potato and Sage Soup

A small amount of bacon contributes to the lovely flavour of this simple soup. Try it with a few crisp croûtons sprinkled over each serving.

Serves 2

2 medium onions
1 medium floury potato, such as Maris Piper
3 fresh sage leaves
2 streaky bacon rashers
2 tsp olive oil
1 tbsp vegetable bouillon powder
1 bay leaf
2 tbsp double cream
Freshly milled salt and black pepper

1. Finely chop the onions. Cut the potato into small dice. Finely chop the sage. Trim the rind from the bacon and chop finely. Put the kettle on to boil.

2. Put the oil and bacon into a large casserole, cover and cook on High for 3 minutes.

3. Stir in the onions and potato, cover and cook on High for 5 minutes.

4. Mix in the chopped sage, vegetable bouillon powder, bay leaf and 150ml/¼ pint boiling water (from the kettle). Cover and cook on High for 10 minutes, stirring once.

5. Remove and discard the bay leaf. Using a hand-held stick blender (or food processor) partially blend the soup to make a thick, chunky consistency, at the same time adding about 300ml/½ pint boiling water (from the kettle).

6. Stir in the cream, season to taste and, if necessary, reheat on High for 1–2 minutes to serve.

Beetroot, Orange and Yogurt Soup

With this soup all the hard work has been done for you, as it's easy to buy the beetroots already cooked and peeled. Just make sure they are not packaged in vinegar.

Serves 2

2 spring onions
225g/8 oz cooked, peeled beetroots
100g/3½ oz mange-touts
1 small orange
1 tsp cornflour
300ml/½ pint unsweetened orange juice
150ml/¼ pint natural yogurt
½ tsp ground coriander
2 tsp bouillon powder
Handful of watercress leaves
Freshly milled salt and black pepper

1. Put the kettle on to boil. Thinly slice the spring onions. Coarsely grate, or finely chop, the beetroots. Cut the mange-touts into long thin strips. Grate the rind from half the orange, cut in half and squeeze the juice from both halves.

2. Put the cornflour into a small bowl or tea cup and add a little orange juice. Mix to a smooth paste and stir in the yogurt.

3. Put the spring onions, beetroots, mange-touts, ground coriander, bouillon powder, orange rind and both juices into a large casserole. Pour over 150ml/¼ pint boiling water (from the kettle). Stir well, cover and cook on High for 5 minutes until the vegetables are soft.

4. Stir in the blended yogurt and watercress leaves, cover and cook on High for 2 minutes.

5. Season if necessary and serve immediately.

Spinach, Rocket and Ham Soup

A soup full of flavour, with peppery rocket, mustard and the smoky flavour of ham. Serve with hot bagels, thinly sliced and toasted.

Serves 2

3 thin slices of cooked smoked ham
2 spring onions
Large handful of spinach leaves
Small handful of rocket leaves
3 walnut halves
1 tsp wholegrain mustard
2 tsp vegetable bouillon powder
150ml/¼ pint unsweetened apple juice
Freshly milled black pepper
2 tbsp natural yogurt
1 tsp olive oil
Bagels, to serve

1. Put the kettle on to boil. Remove any fat from the ham and chop finely. Thinly slice the spring onions. Tear the spinach and rocket leaves into small pieces. Roughly chop the walnuts.

2. Spoon the mustard and bouillon powder into a large casserole and stir in 300ml/½ pint boiling water (from the kettle). Mix in the apple juice, onions, spinach and rocket leaves.

3. Cover and cook on High for 5 minutes. Stir in the ham, cover and cook on High for 2 minutes. If you prefer a smooth soup, whizz with a stick-blender and reheat.

4. Season to taste with black pepper and ladle into serving bowls. Top each portion with a swirl of yogurt, drizzle over a little oil, add a few walnut pieces and serve with the bagels.

Sweet Potato and Tomato Soup with Chorizo

We like to whizz up a can of tomatoes for this, but you could just as easily use the same quantity of passata, or sieved tomatoes. The soup is also good served plain, without the spicy sausage.

Serves 3–4

1 large onion
1 garlic clove
675g/1½ lb sweet potatoes
2 tsp olive oil
1 tsp ground coriander
½ tsp ground cumin
400g can whole tomatoes
About 40g/1½ oz chorizo or similar spicy sausage
1 chicken stock cube or 2 tsp vegetable bouillon powder
Freshly milled salt and black pepper

1. Finely chop the onion and garlic. Peel and finely chop the sweet potatoes. Put the kettle on to boil.

2. Put the onion, garlic and oil into a large casserole. Cover and cook on High for about 3 minutes until soft.

3. Stir in the coriander, cumin and sweet potatoes. Cover and cook on High for 8–10 minutes, stirring once, until soft.

4. Meanwhile, purée the tomatoes until smooth – using a hand-held stick blender or a food processor. Thinly slice or chop the sausage.

5. Stir in the puréed tomatoes, 150ml/¼ pint boiling water (from the kettle) and the stock cube or powder. Cover and cook on High for 5 minutes.

6. Adjust the consistency by stirring in about 300ml/½ pint boiling water (from the kettle). Season to taste.

7. To serve, put some spicy sausage into each serving bowl and ladle the soup over the top.

Oriental Beef Soup

This soup is also delicious made with pork in place of beef. Feel free to add extra ingredients, such as thinly sliced red pepper, finely chopped red chilli or fresh coriander leaves – add them with the spring onions at the beginning of step 4.

Serves 2

100g/3½ oz mushrooms, such as chestnut, shiitake or
   oyster
Slice of fresh root ginger
2 spring onions
100g/3½ oz steak, such as rump or sirloin
3 tbsp soy sauce
2 tbsp medium dry sherry
50g/1¾ oz frozen sweetcorn
100g/3½ oz medium egg noodles
3 tbsp rice vinegar or white wine vinegar
Freshly milled black pepper

1.   Put the kettle on to boil. Thinly slice the mushrooms. Cut the ginger into very fine shreds. Cut the spring onions into thick slices. Thinly slice the steak and then cut the slices into thin shreds.

2.   Put the mushrooms into a casserole. Add the ginger, soy sauce, sherry and 600ml/1 pint boiling water (from the kettle). Cook (no need to cover) on High for 8 minutes.

3.   Add the steak, stirring well to separate the pieces. Stir in the sweetcorn. Break up the noodles and stir in, pushing them under the surface. Cook on High for 3 minutes.

4.   Stir in the spring onions, rice vinegar and a little black pepper. Cook on High for 1–2 minutes until the noodles are soft.

Warm & Salads 4

Salads are typically a summer dish, but warm salads are ideally suited to any season of the year. They can be savoury and spicy and really quite substantial. Cook your personal choice of grains or vegetables, fish or meat, and serve on your favourite selection of salad leaves.

No need to use a frying pan; a small chicken breast, for example, can be microwaved in a small bowl that will be easy to clean. And these salads are so economical on fuel. If cooking for, say, two or three, a different variety of the same salad can easily be made for each person by adding or subtracting an ingredient, or by customising the spices used to suit each individual palate.

Much of the delight of these simple yet impressive dishes comes from the interaction between the cooked food and the salad leaves, which will warm and wilt a little, heightening the flavours as you eat.

Potato and Bacon Salad with Mustard Dressing

This is the dish featured on the front cover. It's very simple to make and tastes just wonderful. Serve it warm or at room temperature, with or without a garnish of baby salad leaves.

Serves 2

600g/1 lb 5 oz baby salad potatoes, such as Charlotte
1 small red onion
1 small red pepper
2 spring onions
2 back bacon rashers .
3 tbsp olive oil
1 tbsp white wine vinegar or lemon juice
2 tsp wholegrain mustard

1. Cut the potatoes in half lengthways and put into a casserole with about 4 tbsp water. Cover and cook on High for about 8 minutes, stirring once, until just tender.

2. Meanwhile, thinly slice the red onion. Halve the red pepper, remove and discard the seeds and stalk, and slice thinly. Slice the spring onions. Cut the bacon rashers into pieces. In a small bowl, mix 1 tbsp oil with the vinegar and mustard.

3. Leave the potatoes in their casserole and allow to stand, covered, while you cook the bacon and vegetables.

4. Put the bacon into a casserole with 2 tbsp oil. Cook (no need to cover) on High for 1½–2 minutes, stirring once, or until the bacon just begins to brown on the edges.

5. Add the red onion and red pepper to the bacon, stirring to coat them with the oil. Cover and cook on High for 1 minute until the vegetables have begun to soften but still have plenty of bite.

6. Drain the potatoes and gently toss them with the bacon mixture, the mustard mixture and the spring onions until well coated.

Minted Bulgur Wheat with Chickpeas

This is lovely just as it is, though you could add extras such as halved cherry tomatoes, stoned olives or some lightly toasted pine nuts. Any leftover salad can be stored in the refrigerator and then served cold.

Serves 2–3

150g/5½ oz bulgur wheat
1 lemon
1 garlic clove
400g can chickpeas
4 tbsp olive oil
Freshly milled salt and black pepper
Handful of fresh mint leaves
Small crisp salad leaves, to serve

1. Put the bulgur wheat into a large bowl and add 500ml/ 18 fl oz cold water. Cover and cook on High for 10 minutes, stirring once. Remove from the microwave, stir, cover and leave to stand for 5–10 minutes until the liquid has been absorbed.

2. Meanwhile, halve the lemon and squeeze out its juice. Crush the garlic. Drain the chickpeas.

3. In another large bowl, mix the oil with the lemon juice, garlic and a little salt and pepper. Stir in the chickpeas. Cook (no need to cover) on High for about 3 minutes until heated through.

4. Stir the bulgur wheat into the chickpea mixture and adjust the seasoning to taste.

5. Just before serving, finely chop the mint leaves and fold them through the salad. Spoon onto crisp salad leaves.

Spiced Tofu with a Crunchy Salad

Tofu made from soya beans is also known as beancurd. Having a neutral or bland quality, it will absorb all the exciting flavours in this substantial salad.

Serves 2

4 spring onions
3 carrots
¼ cos lettuce
1 red pepper
Bunch of radishes
1 garlic clove
Small piece of fresh root ginger
349g packet firm tofu
1 tbsp olive oil
1 tbsp sesame seed oil
2 tbsp soy sauce
2 tsp clear honey
Freshly milled black pepper
2 handfuls of bean sprouts
2 tbsp pine nuts
2 tbsp capers
Hot crusty granary bread, to serve

1. Finely shred the spring onions, carrots, and lettuce. Halve the pepper, remove and discard the seeds and stalk, and slice thinly. Trim and quarter the radishes, crush the garlic and grate the ginger.
2. Drain the tofu, rinse in cold water and dry on kitchen paper. Cut into ten pieces.
3. Pour the olive oil into a casserole and stir in the sesame seed oil, soy sauce, garlic, ginger, honey and a little black pepper. Add the tofu and with a metal spoon carefully turn the pieces until coated with the dressing. If possible leave to marinate for two hours, turning occasionally.
4. In a large bowl mix together the spring onions, carrots, lettuce, red pepper, radishes, bean sprouts, pine nuts and capers. Turn the tofu in the dressing and cook (no need to cover) on High for 3 minutes, turning once until piping hot.
5. Spoon the hot tofu and dressing over the salad, and quickly toss the ingredients together (don't worry if the tofu breaks up a little). Divide between serving bowls and serve immediately with hot crusty granary bread.

Warm Red Beans, Rice and Cheese

Just a few simple ingredients combine to make a lovely gooey mixture. Canned beans and ready-cooked rice help make this one of the speediest of meals. You could of course cook your own rice or use leftover cold rice.

Serves 2

410g can red kidney beans
Small bundle of chives
100g cheese, such as feta or mozzarella
250g packet ready-cooked (microwave) rice, such as brown basmati
1 tbsp wine vinegar
2 tbsp olive oil
Freshly milled salt and pepper
A mixture of crisp salad leaves, to serve

1. Tip the beans into a sieve, rinse and drain them. Snip the chives into short lengths to give about 2 tbsp. Crumble or cut the cheese into small pieces/cubes.

2. Tip the rice into a casserole and stir in the beans, vinegar and oil.

3. Cover and cook on High for about 3 minutes, stirring once, until hot throughout.

4. Season lightly (go easy on the salt when using salty feta cheese) and fold in the cheese and chives.

5. Cover and cook for a further ½–1 minute until the cheese just softens without completely melting.

6. Stir gently and serve immediately piled onto crisp salad leaves.

Hot Goats' Cheese and Avocado Salad

Chèvre or goats' milk cheese has a tart flavour and is delicious when heated until it begins to melt. If you don't care for olives, use pesto or sun-dried tomato paste in place of the tapenade.

Serves 2

2 thick slices of goats' cheese
1 avocado
3 slices of French bread
1 tbsp tapenade (black olive spread)
1 tbsp olive oil
1 tsp walnut oil
2 tsp clear honey
2 tsp sesame seeds
Freshly milled black pepper
Mixed salad leaves

1. Cut each slice of goats' cheese into three segments. Halve the avocado and remove the stone. Scoop out the flesh with a spoon and chop roughly.

2. Halve the bread slices. Spread each piece with a little tapenade, add some chopped avocado and top with a wedge of goats' cheese.

3. Arrange on a wide shallow dish and cook on High (no need to cover) for 2–3 minutes, rearranging the breads once until the cheese is beginning to soften and melt.

4. Meanwhile pour the two oils into a jug. Stir in the honey, sesame seeds and a little black pepper. Cook (no need to cover) on High for 30 seconds until warm.

5. Pile salad leaves onto serving plates, arrange the hot bread pieces on top and drizzle over the warm dressing. Serve immediately.

Hot Sticky Tiger Prawns with Cashew and Cucumber Salad

We sometimes like to make this salad using shell-on prawns – it's quite fun getting sticky peeling off the shells – though you will need to use 300g/10½ oz if you serve it this way. Offer napkins and small bowls of warm water with a slice of lemon floating in each, to clean those sticky fingers at the end of the meal.

Serves 2

Half a cucumber
1 medium red onion
3 celery sticks
2 garlic cloves
1 lime
1 red chilli (see page 10)
Small bunch of dill
Small handful of unsalted cashew nuts
Small bag of salad leaves
3 tbsp olive oil
2 tbsp clear honey
Freshly milled salt and pepper
200g/7 oz shelled, raw tiger prawns
Hot breads, to serve

1. Halve the cucumber lengthways, scoop out the seeds with a small spoon. Cut the cucumber, onion and celery sticks into very thin slices. Crush the garlic cloves. Cut the lime in half and squeeze out the juice. Halve the chilli, remove and discard the seeds and slice thinly. Roughly chop the dill and the cashew nuts.
2. It's important to assemble the salad before you start cooking as the prawns cook very quickly. In a large bowl mix together the onion, celery, cucumber and salad leaves and divide between two serving bowls.
3. In a large casserole mix together the garlic, chilli, oil, lime juice, honey and a little seasoning. Cook (no need to cover) on High for 2 minutes.
4. Add the prawns to the hot mix and stir until coated. Cook on High for 2 minutes or until the prawns are cooked through.
5. Quickly stir in the dill and cashew nuts then spoon over the salad and serve immediately with hot breads.

Thai Spiced Chicken

This works best when served on robust leaves such as spinach and watercress, with some cos lettuce to add some crunch. The fish sauce (nam pla is the Thai name for it) gives the cooked dish a wonderful flavour that is not at all fishy. If you like your food really hot and spicy, add extra chilli powder and add the fresh chilli seeds too.

Serves 2

1 small red onion
Juice of 1 small lemon
1 garlic clove
1 small red chilli (see page 10)
2 skinless chicken breasts, total weight about
  350–375g/12–13 oz
2 tbsp fish sauce
2 tsp oil
2 tsp sugar, preferably molasses
2 tsp cornflour
Generous pinch of chilli powder, or to taste
2–3 tbsp fresh coriander leaves
A selection of salad leaves (see note above)

1. Thinly slice the onion. Halve the lemon and squeeze out its juice. Finely chop or crush the garlic. Thinly slice the chilli, discarding the seeds. Cut the chicken into slices about 5–10mm/¼–½ inch thick.

2. Into a casserole put the garlic, lemon juice, fish sauce, oil, sugar, cornflour and chilli powder. Stir well until smooth. Add the chicken, onion and fresh chilli and stir until well coated. If time allows, cover and leave to stand for 5–10 minutes.

3. Cover and cook on High for about 6 minutes, stirring twice, until the chicken is cooked through and the sauce has thickened. Stir in the coriander leaves.

4. Pile some salad leaves on two serving plates, spoon the hot chicken and its dressing over the top. Don't delay – eat!

Salad of Hot Chicken Livers

Wholegrain mustard, balsamic vinegar and brown sauce add a kick of flavour to this classic salad.

Serves 2

4 spring onions
55g/2 oz button mushrooms
225g/8 oz chicken livers
1 tbsp tomato purée
1 tbsp brown sauce
1 tbsp wholegrain mustard
2 tsp balsamic vinegar
Freshly milled salt and black pepper
Mixed salad leaves
Rocket leaves
Hot garlic bread, to serve

1. Thinly slice the spring onions and mushrooms. Trim and cut the chicken livers into bite-size pieces then rinse in cold water and dry on kitchen paper.

2. In a large casserole mix together the tomato purée, brown sauce, mustard, vinegar and a little seasoning. Stir in the spring onions, mushrooms and chicken livers.

3. Cover and cook on High for 4–5 minutes, stirring once until the chicken livers are cooked.

4. Divide the salad and rocket leaves between two serving plates. Spoon the hot chicken liver mixture over the top and serve immediately with hot garlic bread.

Strictly Vegetables

5

The microwave is ideal for cooking vegetables. When simply cooked, in a little water, many of the nutrients which would be lost into the cooking water of a saucepan are retained in the microwave process. The vegetables emerge with a more concentrated colour and a more intense flavour.

Not only for vegetarians, these dishes are also for anyone fancying a meal without meat or fish, just for a change. Handy, too, if you haven't shopped for a few days, the fridge or the cupboard is a bit bare, and the meat is all gone. Vegetables are flexible and plentiful; and though many are seasonal, there is always a choice to be had.

Some complete meals are included in this section with vegetables taking centre stage, though a side salad, some bread or other accompaniment is often a good idea. In our recipes the vegetables are all cooked and served in their liquid so that your vegetable feast will provide you with maximum nutritional value and pleasure.

Red Cabbage with Sweet Potatoes

Sweet and sour vegetables flavoured with orange, honey and cloves.

Serves 2

1 orange
1 red onion
1 garlic clove
200g/7 oz red cabbage
1 large sweet potato
1 eating apple
2 tsp olive oil
2 tbsp clear honey
2 tbsp red wine vinegar
2 tsp liquid vegetable stock
Pinch of ground cloves

1. Finely grate the rind from the orange, cut in half and squeeze the juice. Finely chop the onion and garlic. Thinly shred the cabbage. Peel and dice the sweet potato. Quarter, core and chop the apple.

2. Put the oil, onion, garlic and red cabbage in a medium casserole. Cover and cook on High for 5 minutes, stirring once.

3. Meanwhile, pour the orange juice into a jug and mix in the orange rind, honey, vinegar, stock and ground cloves.

4. Add the apple and sweet potato to the casserole, pour over the orange mixture and mix well. Cover and cook on High for 5 minutes, or until the vegetables are tender, stirring once.

Coconut Greens

A green vegetarian dish, delicious as an accompaniment for a light lunch or supper, or add a little more stock and coconut milk and serve as a soup with lots of hot bread.

Serves 2

200g/7 oz French beans
Small piece of fresh root ginger
1 garlic clove
Small bunch of fresh mint
½ lime
2 tsp green peppercorns in brine
150ml/¼ pint coconut milk
1 tbsp vegetable bouillon powder
200g/7 oz broad beans
100g/3½ oz mange-touts
Freshly milled salt and black pepper

1. Cut the French beans in half. Grate the ginger and crush the garlic. Pull the mint leaves off the stalks and squeeze the juice from the lime. Drain the peppercorns on kitchen paper.

2. Pour the coconut milk into a medium casserole and stir in the bouillon powder, ginger, garlic, peppercorns and lime juice. Cover and cook on High for 1 minute.

3. Stir in the French beans and broad beans, cover and cook on High for 5 minutes, stirring half way through the cooking time.

4. Stir in the mange-touts and mint leaves, cover and cook on High for about 2 minutes until the vegetables are cooked through. Season, if necessary.

Spiced Vegetable Rice with Chickpeas

This aromatic dish is well worth the long list of ingredients, though the spices could be replaced with curry powder. Serve with some crisp poppadums, mango chutney and raita (plain yogurt with some chopped fresh mint, seasoning and a pinch of sugar stirred in).

Serves 2

100g/3½ oz basmati rice
1 small onion
1 medium carrot
1 medium courgette
400g can chickpeas
3 cardamom pods
1 tbsp oil
3 whole cloves
1 small cinnamon stick
1 tsp cumin seeds
½ tsp ground coriander
½ tsp garam masala
¼ tsp chilli powder
Freshly milled black pepper
2 tsp vegetable bouillon powder
50g/1¾ oz frozen peas

1. Tip the rice into a sieve, rinse thoroughly in cold water and leave to drain. Finely chop the onion, cut the carrot into matchsticks and cut the courgette into small cubes. Drain the chickpeas. Split open and remove the black seeds from the cardamom pods, discarding the husks. Put the kettle on to boil.
2. Put the oil and onion into a large casserole and stir in the cardamom seeds, cloves, cinnamon stick, cumin seeds, coriander, garam masala, chilli powder and a little black pepper. Cover and cook on High for 3 minutes.
3. Stir in the rice, carrot, chickpeas, bouillon powder and 400ml/14 fl oz boiling water (from the kettle). Cook (no need to cover) on High for 9–10 minutes until the rice is just tender and some liquid remains.
4. Stir in the courgette and frozen peas and continue cooking on High for a further 2 minutes.
5. Stir gently, cover and leave to stand for 5 minutes (allowing time for any remaining liquid to be absorbed).

Oriental Vegetables with Smoked Tofu

Like a stir fry that is cooked on the hob, the vegetables need to be added in stages so that they cook perfectly, with each of them retaining some crunch.

Serves 2

3 tbsp soy sauce
2 tsp cornflour
1 tsp clear honey
220g packet smoked tofu
1 medium red onion
1 medium carrot
1 head of broccoli
100g/3½ oz mange-touts
1 garlic clove
1 cm/½ inch piece of fresh root ginger
100g/3½ oz mushrooms, such as chestnut, shiitake or oyster
1 tbsp oil
Handful of bean sprouts – about 150g/5½ oz
Sesame oil (optional)

1. In a small bowl or jug, combine the soy sauce with the cornflour, honey and 1 tbsp water. Drain the tofu, pat dry with kitchen paper and cut into cubes.
2. Thickly slice the onion, thinly slice the carrot on the diagonal. Cut the broccoli into small florets. Halve the mange-touts diagonally. Finely grate the garlic and ginger. Quarter or tear the mushrooms into pieces.
3. Put the oil into a large bowl and stir in the onion, carrot, garlic and ginger. Cover and cook on High for 4 minutes.
4. Stir in the broccoli florets, mange-touts and mushrooms, cover and cook on High for 2 minutes.
5. Add the soy sauce mixture, stirring, and then the tofu. Cover and cook on High for 1 minute.
6. Finally, stir in the bean sprouts. Cover and cook on High for 2–3 minutes until just softened and the sauce is cooked (you should not be able to taste the cornflour). Serve immediately, sprinkled with a little sesame oil if liked.

Potatoes with Blue Cheese and Cheddar

The idea for this simple recipe came from the French dish of potatoes and cheese that is baked in the oven. We enjoy it straight from the microwave, though you could of course pop it under a hot grill to brown the top before serving – make sure the dish is flameproof.

Serves 2

1 small onion
500g/1 lb 2 oz waxy potatoes, such as Charlotte
15g/½ oz butter
2 tbsp dry white vermouth or wine
50g/1¾ oz mature Cheddar cheese
50g/1¾ oz creamy blue cheese, such as Cambozola
About 2 tbsp milk
Freshly milled salt and black pepper
About 2 tbsp walnut pieces

1. Thinly slice the onion. Cut the potatoes into cubes measuring about 1cm/½ inch.

2. Put the onion and butter into a medium casserole, cover and cook on High for 3 minutes until softened.

3. Stir in the potatoes and the vermouth or wine. Cover and cook for about 8 minutes, stirring once or twice, until the potatoes are just tender.

4. Meanwhile, cut both types of cheese into small pieces.

5. When the potatoes are just cooked, stir in the cheeses and milk. Cover and cook on High for 2 minutes.

6. Stir the melted cheese through the potatoes and season with salt and pepper. Cover and leave to stand for a few minutes before serving. Sprinkle each portion with walnuts.

Vegetables in Peanut Sauce

If you like the sauce known as satay, you are sure to like this. It is rich and warming – an ideal winter dish made with root vegetables. Serve it in bowls with chunks of crusty bread alongside.

Serves 2

1 medium onion
1 celery stick
200g/7 oz carrots
200g/7 oz waxy potatoes, such as Charlotte
200g/7 oz sweet potato
200g/7 oz parsnip
1 lime
1 tsp olive oil
2 generous tbsp unsweetened crunchy peanut butter
2 tbsp soy sauce
1 tsp clear honey
1 tsp sesame oil
Chopped fresh coriander leaves, to serve

1. Finely chop the onion and thinly slice the celery. Cut the carrots, potatoes, sweet potato and parsnip into chunks measuring about 2cm/¾ inch. Cut the lime in half and squeeze out the juice.

2. Put the olive oil, onion and celery into a large casserole, cover and cook on High for 3 minutes until softened.

3. Stir in the carrots, potatoes, sweet potato and parsnip. Cover and cook on High for about 8 minutes, stirring once, until just tender.

4. Meanwhile, combine the peanut butter with the soy sauce, honey, lime juice, sesame oil and 100ml/3½ fl oz water.

5. Stir the peanut sauce into the hot vegetables, stirring gently until coated. Cook on High (no need to cover) for 2 minutes.

6. Use a large spoon to turn the vegetables gently until the sauce thickens slightly. Serve with chopped coriander leaves sprinkled over.

Red Peppers with Avocado, Rice and Red Pesto

A delicious, colourful dish. Buy ready-cooked rice or cook your own (see page 103). Serve with salad and hot garlic bread.

Serves 2

2 large red peppers
2 shallots
1 small avocado
2 tsp lime juice
1 tbsp olive oil
100g/3½ oz cooked long grain rice
2 tbsp red pesto

1. Cut the peppers in half, remove and discard the seeds, but leave the stalk intact. Finely chop the shallots. Cut the avocado in half, remove the stone, peel away the skin, slice the flesh into a bowl and pour over the lime juice (to prevent it turning brown).

2. Put the oil and shallots in a bowl, cover and cook on High for 3 minutes until softened.

3. Gently stir in the rice, pesto, avocado and lime juice.

4. Put the pepper halves into a large casserole and fill with the rice mixture. Pour 2 tbsp cold water around the peppers.

5. Cover and cook on High for about 4 minutes until the filling is piping hot. Serve immediately.

Aubergines with Pine Nuts and Paneer Cheese

Paneer or pannir is an Indian cheese with a texture rather like tofu. Don't worry if you can't find it, this recipe works well with feta, mozzarella or Cheddar cheese.

Serves 2

2 small courgettes
100g/3½ oz paneer cheese
Small bunch of fresh tarragon
2 pimentos, drained
2 medium aubergines
1 tbsp lemon juice
1 tbsp oil, plus extra for brushing
2 tsp vegetable bouillon powder
2 tbsp sultanas
100g/3½ oz pine nuts
Freshly milled salt and black pepper

1. Coarsely grate the courgettes. Cut the paneer cheese into small cubes and roughly chop the tarragon and pimentos. Cut the aubergines in half lengthways. With a spoon, scoop out some of the flesh from each half to leave a hollow. Brush the insides of the shells with a little lemon juice to prevent browning and brush the outsides with a little oil. Finely chop the scooped-out aubergine flesh.

2. Put the aubergine shells into a large casserole and pour 2 tbsp cold water around them. Cover and cook on High for 2–3 minutes, or until the shells are almost cooked, but not too soft (otherwise they may collapse).

3. Put the bouillon powder into a medium bowl and stir in 4 tbsp water. Mix in the oil and chopped aubergine. Cover and cook on High for 3 minutes.

4. Stir the grated courgettes into the aubergine mixture, cover and cook for 2 minutes.

5. Mix in the pimentos, paneer cheese, sultanas, pine nuts, chopped tarragon and a little seasoning. Spoon the mixture into the aubergine shells. Cover and cook on High for 4 minutes until the filling is piping hot. Serve immediately.

Fasta Pasta, Rice & Grains

6

Pasta comes in a plenitude of shapes, and rice and grains in a multitude of varieties. They all add texture and interest to a dish, and they absorb and enhance the flavours of surrounding sauces and dressings. Generally, they take as long to cook in the microwave as by conventional means, but it is such a convenient way to cook them, and so clean. There is no worry about burning the food by boiling the pan dry. Always use a large, deep container to allow plenty of room for the contents to boil up.

Within the recipes we explain the basic method for cooking pasta (see pages 59 and 60), noodles (pages 61 and 62) and couscous (page 65). Meanwhile, basic instructions for rice appear on page 103. Then, with this advice in mind, try your hand at our recipes for red rice and risotto rice, spaghetti and pasta shapes, egg noodles and rice noodles, couscous and polenta. They are so straightforward yet so delicious. And if you still want more, we've included other dishes using rice and grains elsewhere in our book. You can find these other recipes by searching the index.

Pasta in Creamy Leek and Parmesan Sauce

Here is the basic method for cooking pasta in the microwave. The sauce is cooked while the pasta stands, then the two are stirred together.

Serves 2

2 large leeks
200g/7 oz pasta shapes, such as penne or twists
4 tbsp vegetable stock or dry white vermouth or wine
15g/½ oz butter
1 medium tomato
Freshly milled salt and pepper
3 tbsp double cream
About 25g/1 oz freshly grated Parmesan cheese, plus extra for serving

1. Put the kettle on to boil. Thinly slice the leeks.

2. Put the pasta into a large casserole and pour over sufficient boiling water (from the kettle), to cover it by about 5cm/2 inches. Stir well. Cook (do not cover) on High for about 10 minutes, stirring once until just soft. Stir, cover and leave to stand while you cook the sauce.

3. Put the leeks into a casserole with the stock or vermouth or wine and butter. Cover and cook on High for 8–10 minutes, stirring once, until very soft.

4. Meanwhile, halve the tomato, remove and discard the seeds and chop the flesh finely.

5. Season the leeks with salt and pepper and stir in the cream. Cover and cook on High for 2–3 minutes.

6. Stir in the Parmesan cheese and chopped tomato. Adjust the seasoning to taste if necessary.

7. Drain the pasta and stir into the sauce. Serve with extra Parmesan cheese for sprinkling over.

Spaghetti with Herbs and Smoked Salmon

We've used smoked salmon in the sauce but you can use a drained can of tuna or salmon, or cooked flaked trout. Fennel as a vegetable adds a lovely aniseed flavour.

Serves 2

1 small fennel bulb
1 small lemon
8 baby plum tomatoes
6 black olives, stoned
Small bunch of fresh dill
Small bunch of fresh chives
200g/7 oz smoked salmon
200g/7 oz spaghetti
2 tsp olive oil
Freshly milled salt and black pepper

1. Put the kettle on to boil. Finely chop the fennel bulb. Grate the rind from the lemon, cut in half and squeeze the juice. Halve the tomatoes and olives. Finely chop the dill and chives. Cut the smoked salmon into very thin strips.

2. Put the spaghetti into a large casserole, breaking it in half to fit. Pour over sufficient boiling water (from the kettle) to cover it by about 5cm/2 inches and stir well. Cook (do not cover) on High for about 10 minutes, stirring once until soft. Stir, cover and leave to stand while you make the sauce.

3. Put the oil, fennel, lemon rind and juice into a casserole, cover and cook on High for 6 minutes until softened, stirring once.

4. Stir the tomatoes and olives into the fennel mixture, cover and cook on High for 2 minutes.

5. Add the smoked salmon to the vegetables and season if necessary. Cover and cook on Medium for 1 minute.

6. Drain the pasta, carefully fold in the herbs and salmon mixture then serve immediately.

Rice Noodles with Seafood and Black Bean Sauce

Rice noodles are a useful store-cupboard ingredient. They are pre-cooked so only need soaking in boiling water to soften them before use.

Serves 2

200g/7 oz rice noodles
3 spring onions
2 garlic cloves
1 large carrot
100g/3½ oz French beans
1 small red pepper
Small bunch of fresh coriander
250g/9 oz mixed shelled seafood, such as mussels,
**   prawns, squid or skinless fish fillets**
2 tsp sesame oil
2 tsp liquid chicken stock
2 tbsp light soy sauce
2 tbsp black bean sauce
2 tbsp sesame seeds
Freshly milled salt and black pepper
Lemon wedges, to serve

1. Put the kettle on to boil. Put the rice noodles into a large bowl and pour over boiling water (from the kettle) to cover. Leave to stand, stirring occasionally to separate the noodles.
2. Cut the spring onions, garlic and carrot into very thin strips. Halve the French beans if they are long. Cut the pepper in half, remove and discard the seeds and stalk, and chop finely. Pull the coriander leaves from the stalks. Cut fish fillets (if using) into bite-size pieces.
3. Stir the sesame oil, chicken stock, soy sauce, black bean sauce and 1 tbsp water into a large casserole. Add the spring onions, garlic, carrot, French beans and red pepper. Cover and cook on High for 6 minutes until softened, stirring twice during the cooking.
4. Stir in the seafood, cover and cook on Medium-High for about 2 minutes until the fish is just cooked.
5. Drain the noodles and cook on High (no need to cover) for 1 minute until piping hot. Stir into the seafood mixture with the coriander leaves and sesame seeds, season if necessary and serve immediately with lemon wedges.

Beef Teriyaki

The vegetables remain slightly crisp while the beef stays beauti-
fully tender. It looks good served in shallow bowls. Anyone who
appreciates spicy food will enjoy sprinkling the finished dish with
a little chilli sauce.

Serves 2

1 medium leek
1 medium carrot
1 small red pepper
1cm/½ inch fresh root ginger
100g/3½ oz mushrooms, such as chestnut or oyster
250g/9 oz lean rump steak
2 tbsp tamari or soy sauce, plus extra for serving
¼ tsp five-spice powder
½ tsp sugar
100g/3½ oz dried medium egg noodles
2 tsp vegetable bouillon powder
1 tsp sesame seeds

1. Thinly slice the leek and the carrot. Halve the red pepper, remove and discard the seeds and stalk, and slice thinly. Finely grate the ginger. Thickly slice the mushrooms. Put the kettle on to boil.
2. Cut the steak into thin strips, preferably across the grain. Put into a bowl and stir in the tamari or soy sauce, five-spice powder and sugar. Set aside.
3. Put the egg noodles into a shallow bowl, breaking them slightly if necessary, and pour over 425ml/¾ pint boiling water (from the kettle). Stir gently to start separating the strands, then leave to stand.
4. Put the leek, carrot, pepper, ginger and vegetable bouillon powder into a large casserole and add 1 tbsp water. Cover and cook on High for 3 minutes.
5. Stir the steak and its liquid into the vegetables, cover and cook for 2 minutes.
6. Stir to separate the beef slices, then add the mushrooms and the noodles and their liquid, gently stirring in. Cover and cook on High for about 3 minutes until the noodles are soft and the beef is just cooked. Stir gently once more, cover and leave to stand for a minute or two before serving, sprinkled with the sesame seeds. Hand round extra tamari or soy sauce if wished.

Chicken in Saffron Rice

Saffron adds its distinctive flavour to this creamy risotto-like dish. Serve it in shallow bowls, maybe with a crisp green salad, tossed in a little oil-and-vinegar dressing, alongside.

Serves 2

1 medium onion
1 garlic clove
Pinch of saffron threads
4 large or 6 small boneless, skinless chicken thighs
1 tbsp olive oil
150g/5½ oz risotto rice, such as arborio
1 chicken stock cube
100ml/3½ fl oz dry white vermouth or wine
Freshly milled salt and pepper
Chopped fresh parsley, to serve

1. Put the kettle on to boil. Finely chop the onion and garlic. Put the saffron into a small bowl, crush it lightly with the back of a small spoon, stir in 2 tbsp boiling water (from the kettle) and leave to stand. Cut each chicken thigh into about three pieces.

2. Put the oil into a large casserole with the onion and garlic. Cover and cook on High for 3 minutes.

3. Stir the rice into the onion mixture, cover and cook on High for 2 minutes.

4. Dissolve the stock cube in 250ml/9 fl oz boiling water (from the kettle). Stir into the rice with the vermouth or wine and the saffron mixture. Add the chicken, pushing the pieces beneath the surface. Cover and cook on High for about 15 minutes, stirring two or three times, until the rice is tender but still retains a 'bite', the chicken is cooked and there is still some liquid remaining.

5. Season to taste, stir, cover and leave to stand for 5 minutes until almost all the liquid has been absorbed and the rice is coated in a creamy sauce. Serve spooned into warmed serving bowls, sprinkled with a little chopped fresh parsley.

Red Rice with Chorizo Sausage

Red rice with its nutty texture is a good partner for the robust flavours of the spicy red Spanish sausage – chorizo.

Serves 2

1 red onion
200g/7 oz chorizo sausage, in one piece
Small bunch of flat-leaf parsley
100g/3½ oz Camargue red rice
2 tsp vegetable bouillon powder
Freshly milled salt and black pepper

1. Put the kettle on to boil. Thinly slice the onion and dice the chorizo. Roughly chop the parsley. Tip the rice into a sieve, rinse thoroughly in cold water and leave to drain.

2. Put the rice into a large casserole, pour over 300ml/½ pint boiling water (from the kettle) and stir in the vegetable bouillon powder.

3. Cover and cook on High for 9 minutes or until the rice is just tender and some liquid remains. Leave to stand for 5 minutes – this allows time for any remaining liquid to be absorbed.

4. Put the onion and chorizo into a medium casserole. Cover and cook on High for 3 minutes, stirring occasionally until the onion has softened in the juices from the chorizo sausage.

5. Stir the sausage mixture and parsley into the cooked rice. Season if necessary and serve immediately.

Mushroom Couscous

Couscous made from cracked cereal grains is another good store-cupboard stand-by. Most couscous is pre-cooked – just cover it in boiling water, leave to soak, drain and with a fork separate the grains before using. Try it cold in salads. Here it's served warm with herbs and mushrooms.

Serves 2

1 yellow pepper
1 red chilli (see page 10)
Small bunch of fresh mint leaves
Small bunch of fresh flat-leaved parsley
Small bunch of chives
200g/7 oz mixed mushrooms, such as shiitake, chestnut or
**   oyster**
4 ready-to-eat dried apricots
½ lemon
200g/7 oz couscous
1 tbsp olive oil
1 tbsp liquid vegetable stock
1 tsp garlic paste
Small handful of sultanas
Freshly milled salt and black pepper

1. Put the kettle on to boil. Cut the pepper and chilli in half, remove and discard the seeds and stalks, and chop finely. Pull the mint leaves from the stalks and finely chop the parsley and chives. Cut the mushrooms into bite-size pieces and thinly slice the apricots. Squeeze the juice from the lemon.
2. Put the couscous into a large bowl and pour over boiling water (from the kettle) to cover. Leave to stand, stirring occasionally.
3. Pour 150ml/¼ pint boiling water (from the kettle) into a medium casserole and stir in the oil, stock, garlic paste, lemon juice, yellow pepper, chilli, apricots and sultanas. Cover and cook on High for 6 minutes until the apricots are tender.
4. Stir in the mushrooms, cover and cook on High for about 3 minutes until cooked through.
5. Drain the couscous, return it to the bowl and cook on High (no need to cover) for 3 minutes until piping hot. Stir into the mushroom mixture, mix in all the herbs and season if necessary. Cover and leave to stand for 5 minutes for the flavours to develop. Serve warm.

Polenta with Aubergine and Red Pepper Sauce

Here we give the basic method for cooking polenta or cornmeal. Serve it as an accompaniment or with a sauce such as this one. The hot cooked polenta could also be spread in an even layer in a shallow dish and left to cool – to be cut into shapes when firm, brushed with butter or oil and browned under a hot grill.

Serves 2 as a main dish, 4 as a starter

400g can whole plum tomatoes
1 small onion
1 garlic clove
1 small-to-medium aubergine
1 small red pepper
2 tsp olive oil
1 generous tsp dried oregano leaves
1 heaped tsp vegetable bouillon powder
Freshly milled salt and black pepper
125g/4½ oz polenta (fine or medium cornmeal)
15–25g/½–1 oz butter
Freshly grated or shaved Parmesan cheese, to serve

1. Tip the tomatoes into a sieve and, with your hand, break them up into pieces, allowing the liquid to drain away. Finely chop the onion and garlic. Cut the aubergine into small dice. Halve the red pepper, remove and discard the seeds and stalk, and cut into small pieces. Put the kettle on to boil.
2. To make the sauce, put the oil, onion, garlic, aubergine and oregano into a casserole, cover and cook on High for 5 minutes until soft. Stir in the red pepper, tomatoes, vegetable bouillon powder and seasoning. Cover and cook on High for 5 minutes until very soft and thick. Leave to stand, covered, while you cook the polenta.
3. Pour 750ml/1¼ pints boiling water (from the kettle) into a large bowl or casserole. Tip the polenta into the water and stir well. Cover and cook on High, stirring occasionally, until very thick (with a consistency similar to mashed potato) – expect instant polenta to take 8–10 minutes and traditional varieties up to 20 minutes.
4. Reheat the sauce on High for 1–2 minutes. Meanwhile, stir the butter into the hot polenta.
5. Serve the polenta with the sauce spooned over and topped with a little Parmesan cheese.

It's a Wrap! 7

Wraps are a popular choice today. You see them everywhere on the high street, in shops and cafés; they are a stylish edible accessory for people constantly on the move. But why not prepare them at home? You can buy the wraps and make the fillings yourself – then you can be sure that the filling is fresh, made with healthy ingredients, and will be as tasty as it should be.

There are endless filling-and-wrap combinations. Pitta breads, flatbreads, soft tortillas, naan breads and pancakes are all excellent for wraps. Put the wrap(s) on a plate, cover loosely with clear film and gently warm them in the microwave on a Medium-Low power. What could be simpler?

Wraps make a great stand-by snack, and they can come in very useful for feeding those unexpected visitors. In fact, you might find your visitors start to drop in more often just to try your latest filling-and-wrap combination.

Falafels with Sesame Seed and Yogurt Dressing

A hands-on dish. Falafels and wraps with fascinating flavours.

Serves 2

2 garlic cloves
Small bunch of fresh coriander
2 tbsp sesame seeds
200g can chickpeas
½ tsp ground cardamom
½ tsp ground coriander
1 tsp lemon juice
Freshly milled salt and black pepper
2 tsp oil
1 tsp clear honey
150ml/¼ pint natural yogurt
Wraps of your choice (see page 67)
Shredded lettuce, to serve

1. Crush the garlic cloves and chop the coriander. Using a pestle and mortar or a food processor, crush the sesame seeds. Drain the chickpeas into a bowl.

2. With a fork or a stick-blender crush the chickpeas to a thick paste. Stir in half of the garlic, half of the chopped coriander, ground cardamom and ground coriander, lemon juice and a little seasoning.

3. With damp hands, shape the mixture into six balls to make the falafels and flatten slightly. Brush with a little oil and lift onto a shallow dish. Cook on High for 4 minutes, turning once until piping hot and cooked through.

4. To make the dressing, stir the remaining garlic and chopped coriander, the honey and the sesame seeds into the yogurt and season. If the mixture seems too thick, thin with a little cold water.

5. Heat your chosen wraps (see page 67), fill with the shredded lettuce, falafels and a spoonful of dressing, and serve immediately.

Fresh Spinach, Beans and Feta

This mixture is also delicious served on hot toast or on toasted garlic bread. It can be served hot, warm or cold.

Serves 2

1 large onion
2 tbsp olive oil
Good pinch of sugar
Two large handfuls of fresh spinach leaves (total weight about 175g/6 oz)
1 garlic clove
400g can beans, such as borlotti, haricot or black eye
About 100g/3½ oz feta cheese
Freshly milled black pepper
Wraps of your choice (see page 67)
Lemon wedges, to serve

1. Thinly slice the onion and put into a large casserole. Add 1 tbsp oil and the sugar. Cover and cook on High for 8–10 minutes, stirring once, until very soft.

2. Meanwhile, wash, drain and dry the spinach leaves. Crush the garlic clove. Drain the beans.

3. Stir the garlic and beans into the hot onion, then add the spinach. Cover and cook on High for about 3 minutes, stirring once, until the spinach has just wilted.

4. Crumble in the feta cheese, season with black pepper and add the remaining 1 tbsp olive oil. Stir the mixture gently until well combined.

5. Heat your chosen wraps (see page 67), fill with the bean mixture and serve with lemon wedges for squeezing over.

Artichoke and Blue Cheese

Just five ingredients go into this filling, though a few pieces of walnut or chopped crisp apple wouldn't go amiss – just sprinkle over the filling before serving.

Serves 2

280g jar artichokes in oil
100g/3½ oz blue cheese, such as Gorgonzola
Handful of baby spinach leaves
1–2 tbsp chopped fresh chives
Freshly milled black pepper
Wraps of your choice (see page 67)

1. Tip the artichokes into a sieve and leave to drain for a few minutes. Cut the cheese into cubes. Roughly chop the spinach. Halve or quarter the artichokes.

2. Put the artichokes into a bowl and cook (no need to cover) on High for 1 minute.

3. Stir in the cheese and spinach and cook on High for 1–2 minutes or until the cheese has just melted and the spinach has wilted. Stir in the chives and season with black pepper.

4. Heat your chosen wraps (see page 67), fill with the artichoke mixture and serve immediately.

Hot Spiced Trout

Five-spice powder is a mix of cinnamon, star anise, cloves, fennel seeds and Sichuan peppercorns and features in Chinese cooking. Using this flavour mix is a speedy way of adding punch to a recipe.

Serves 2

3 spring onions
5 small plum tomatoes
2 trout fillets, skinned
1 tsp Chinese five-spice powder
1 tbsp chilli oil
Freshly milled black pepper
Wraps of your choice (see page 67)
Handful of spinach leaves
Parmesan shavings, to serve
Thick Greek yogurt, to serve (optional)

1. Thinly slice the spring onions and quarter the tomatoes. Cut each trout fillet diagonally into three pieces.

2. In a medium casserole mix together the five-spice powder, chilli oil and a little black pepper. Carefully turn the spring onions, tomatoes and fish pieces in the mixture.

3. Cover and cook on High for 2–3 minutes or until the fish is almost cooked through. Leave to stand, covered, for 2 minutes to allow the trout to finish cooking.

4. Heat your chosen wraps (see page 67), fill with the spinach leaves and top with the trout mixture. Add a few Parmesan shavings and a little yogurt (if using). Serve immediately.

Salmon with Mustardy Vegetables

Works well with trout fillets and firm white fish such as monkfish or halibut.

Serves 2

1 medium leek
1 medium carrot
250g/9oz skinless salmon fillet
25g/1 oz butter
1 tbsp wholegrain mustard
Wraps of your choice (see page 67)
Fresh chives
Crisp salad leaves or watercress sprigs, to serve
Lime or lemon wedges, to serve

1. Cut the leek into 5cm/2 inch lengths, then cut each piece lengthways into quarters to make strips. Cut the carrot into similar lengths and cut into sticks slightly thicker than a matchstick. Cut the salmon into strips about 5–10mm/¼–½ inch thick.

2. Put the leek, carrot and butter into a casserole. Cover and cook on High, stirring once, for 5 minutes until soft.

3. Stir the mustard into the hot vegetables and, when coated, stir in the salmon. Cover and cook on High for 2–3 minutes until the salmon is almost cooked through.

4. Leave to stand, covered, for 2 minutes to allow the salmon to finish cooking.

5. Meanwhile, heat your chosen wraps (see page 67) and fill with the salmon mixture, snipping some chives over the top. Serve with crisp salad leaves or watercress sprigs and lime or lemon wedges for squeezing over.

Sticky Cajun Chicken

A dish to get stuck into with relish.

Serves 2

1 medium red onion
2 celery sticks
1 green pepper
200g/7 oz boneless, skinless chicken
½ tsp ground cardamom
½ tsp ground coriander
Pinch of cayenne pepper
3 tbsp tomato ketchup
1 tsp chilli paste
1 tbsp molasses or dark brown sugar
1 tsp lemon juice
Freshly milled salt and black pepper
Wraps of your choice (see page 67)

1. Thinly slice the onion and celery sticks. Cut the pepper in half, remove and discard the seeds and stalk, and slice thinly. Cut the chicken into thin strips.

2. In a medium casserole mix together the ground cardamom and coriander, cayenne pepper, tomato ketchup, chilli paste, molasses or brown sugar, lemon juice and a little seasoning. Add the chicken and mix until thoroughly coated with the paste. If you have time, leave to stand for 30 minutes for the flavours to develop.

3. Cover and cook on Medium-High for about 5 minutes, stirring twice, or until the chicken is cooked through.

4. Heat your chosen wraps (see page 67), fill with some of the onion, celery and green pepper. Top with the chicken and its sauce, then serve immediately.

Pork with Satay Sauce

*We have made this recipe with pork, but it works equally well
with chicken breast. Chinese pancakes (the sort normally served
with crispy duck) make particularly suitable wraps.*

Serves 2

2 spring onions
1 small garlic clove
2 tbsp unsweetened peanut butter
2 tbsp soy sauce
1 tbsp wine vinegar
2 tsp dark brown sugar
1 tsp sweet chilli sauce
250g/9 oz pork loin/fillet
Wraps of your choice (see page 67)
Shredded lettuce, to serve
Thinly sliced cucumber, to serve (optional)

1. Thinly slice the spring onions and set aside. Finely chop or
    crush the garlic, put into a medium casserole and stir in
    the peanut butter, soy sauce, vinegar, sugar and chilli
    sauce. Slice the pork into discs about 5mm/¼ inch thick
    and stir into the sauce mixture until well coated.

2. Cover and cook on Medium-High for about 5 minutes,
    stirring twice, or until the pork is cooked through.

3. With a slotted spoon, lift the pork onto a plate.

4. Stir half the spring onions into the sauce and cook (do not
    cover) on High for 2–3 minutes until reduced and very
    thick (you will need to be able to spread it on the wraps).

5. Heat your chosen wraps (see page 67). Spread a little of
    the sauce on each wrap, add some pork, shredded
    lettuce, cucumber (if using) and the remaining spring
    onions. Roll or fold up and serve immediately.

Chilli Beef with Horseradish Dressing

Horseradish and chilli add both heat and spice to tender strips of beef. In place of the beef and horseradish try lamb and mint sauce or pork and apple purée.

Serves 2

2 spring onions
1 small courgette
1 red chilli (see page 10)
2 oyster mushrooms
200g/7 oz lean beef steak
2 tsp horseradish sauce
2 tbsp thick Greek yogurt
2 tsp olive oil
Freshly milled salt and black pepper
Wraps of your choice (see page 67)
Shredded lettuce, to serve

1. Thinly shred the spring onions and courgette. Halve the chilli, remove and discard the seeds, and slice thinly. If the mushrooms are large, tear them into bite-size pieces. Cut the beef into thin slivers.

2. In a small bowl mix together the horseradish sauce and yogurt.

3. Put the beef into a medium casserole and stir in the oil, chilli and mushrooms. Cover and cook on High for 5 minutes, stirring half-way through the cooking time, until the beef is cooked to your liking. Season, if necessary.

4. Heat your chosen wraps (see page 67), fill with the beef mixture, some shredded spring onion, courgette and lettuce. Add a spoonful of the horseradish dressing and serve immediately.

Smart Dining
for One & Two

8

Smart dining on a small scale is often daunting. Too many pots and pans are needed (all that washing up), and a disproportionate amount of effort. So how can you achieve great results while managing to relax in the run-up to your meal or having more time to spend with your dining companion?

This is just how your microwave can surprise you. Who says that classy, stylish, elegant gourmet food for one or two cannot be made in a microwave? Our recipes aim to disprove this assumption. It is always tempting, when cooking on this scale, to include some luxury items, and we have certainly not resisted this temptation. So impress your guest or partner, or simply indulge yourself, by trying our recipes for pork loin (see page 82), venison fillet (see page 85) or green-lipped mussels (see page 80).

Seafood Gumbo

This Creole-style fish stew contains okra, or ladies' fingers, which helps to thicken the sauce. We use white fish, smoked fish, salmon and prawns, but try adding cooked mussels, cockles and/or squid rings too. Serve with crusty bread.

Serves 2

400g can whole plum tomatoes
1 small onion
1 garlic clove
1 medium sweet potato (about 200g/7 oz)
1 small red or green pepper
75g/2¾ okra
2 tsp oil
1½ tsp ground coriander
1 tsp chilli powder
½ tsp turmeric
2 bay leaves (optional)
150ml/¼ pint fish or vegetable stock
350g/12 oz mixture of skinless fish (cod, smoked haddock and salmon) and raw shelled prawns
Freshly milled salt and black pepper
Chopped fresh parsley, to serve

1. Tip the tomatoes into a sieve and, with your hand, break them up into pieces, allowing the liquid to drain away. Finely chop the onion and garlic. Peel the sweet potato and cut into small cubes. Halve the red or green pepper, remove and discard the seeds and stalk, and cut into small pieces. Trim off and discard the stalk ends from the okra and cut the rest into thick slices.
2. Put the oil, onion and garlic into a casserole, cover and cook for 3 minutes until soft.
3. Add the sweet potato, red or green pepper and okra. Stir in the coriander, chilli, turmeric, bay leaves (if using), tomatoes and stock. Cover and cook on High for about 10 minutes, stirring once or twice, until the sweet potato is soft.
4. Stir in the fish, cover and cook on High for 3 minutes, stirring gently once, or until the fish is just cooked.
5. Season lightly with salt and pepper, cover and leave to stand for a few minutes before serving (during which time the fish will finish cooking). Sprinkle some chopped parsley over each serving.

Surf and Turf Kebabs

Monkfish and turkey kebabs, full of extra flavour from the marinade of lemon grass and ginger. Serve with the sauce on the side, lemon wedges, salad and hot garlic bread.

Serves 2

200g/7 oz monkfish
200g/7 oz skinless turkey steak
8 button mushrooms

Marinade
Small piece of fresh lemon grass
Small piece of fresh root-ginger
1 tbsp dry white wine
1 tbsp pesto
1 tsp balsamic vinegar
Freshly milled white pepper

1 small red pepper
1 small lemon

Sauce
2 tsp cornflour
150ml/¼ pint dry white wine

1. Cut both the monkfish and the turkey steak into eight bite-sized pieces. Trim the mushroom stalks level with the base of the caps.
2. Prepare the marinade: finely chop the lemon grass, finely grate the root-ginger and put both into a wide bowl. Stir in the white wine, pesto, balsamic vinegar and a little white pepper. Add the monkfish, turkey and the mushrooms, turning them in the marinade until coated. If time allows, cover, chill and leave to marinate for an hour to allow the flavours to develop.
3. Meanwhile, cut the red pepper in half, remove and discard the seeds and stalks, and cut into eight pieces. Slice the lemon into wedges.
4. With a slotted spoon lift the monkfish, turkey and mushrooms out of the marinade. Thread them, with the pepper, onto four wooden kebab skewers, leaving a small gap between each piece.

5. Arrange the skewers on a large plate or shallow dish, like the spokes of a wheel. Cover loosely and cook on High for 8–9 minutes, rearranging them half-way through the cooking time and brushing with extra marinade, until cooked through and piping hot.

6. Lift the kebabs from the dish, cover and stand whilst you make the sauce. Put the cornflour into a heatproof jug, blend to a smooth paste with a little of the wine, then add the rest of the wine, the remaining marinade and the cooking juices. Make up to 300ml/½ pint with cold water. Cook (no need to cover) on High for about 2 minutes, whisking half-way through the cooking time until piping hot and thickened.

Tuna Steak with Pistachio Nut Topping

Tuna is a 'meaty' fish with no waste. Serve with noodles, new potatoes, rice or salad. We prefer tuna served a little pink in the middle; if you prefer it cooked all the way through, cook for about 50 seconds extra.

Serves 1

8 shelled, skinned pistachio nuts
2 sprigs of fresh dill
A few fresh chive sprigs
1 tsp olive oil
1 tsp wholegrain mustard
Freshly milled black pepper
150g/5½ oz tuna steak
Lemon wedge, to serve

1. Finely chop the pistachio nuts, dill and chives.
2. In a small bowl, mix together the oil, mustard, pistachio nuts, dill, chives and a little black pepper.
3. Put the tuna steak on a plate or shallow dish and spread the pistachio paste over the top. Cover and cook on Medium-High for about 2 minutes until barely cooked. Leave to stand, covered for 2 minutes.
4. Serve the tuna with the juices spooned over and a lemon wedge on the side.

Green-lipped Mussels with Vermouth

These large 'meaty' New Zealand mussels are sold in a half shell. Perfect for this topping made with parsley, lime, vermouth and Thai fish sauce. Serve with a watercress salad as a starter or light lunch dish.

Serves 2

3 sprigs of flat-leaf parsley
½ small lime
9 green-lipped mussels
1 tsp Thai fish sauce
1 tbsp dry white vermouth
Freshly milled black pepper

1. Remove the leaves from the parsley stalks and chop finely. Squeeze the juice from the lime.

2. With a sharp knife, loosen the mussels from their shells. Carefully rinse the shells and the mussels in cold water to remove any bits of grit, shell or hairy 'beard'. Drain on kitchen paper and return the mussels to the shells.

3. In a small bowl, mix together the lime juice, fish sauce, vermouth, chopped parsley and a little black pepper.

4. Arrange the mussels in their shells around the edges of a large plate. Spoon a little of the sauce mixture over each mussel.

5. Cook on High (no need to cover) for about 1½ minutes, rearranging them half-way through the cooking time until piping hot.

Prawn and Potato Chermoula

Chermoula is a North African paste which is good used as a marinade. Typical ingredients include olive oil, garlic, cumin, hot spices like chilli or cayenne, lemon juice and sometimes saffron. A dressed salad of crisp lettuce, cucumber and tomato is all that is needed alongside. For large appetites, serve a warmed flat bread for tearing up and mopping up the lovely sauce.

Serves 2

1 garlic clove
250g/9 oz baby potatoes, such as Charlotte
2 spring onions
Fresh coriander leaves
Fresh flat-parsley leaves
Pinch of saffron threads (optional)
1 tbsp olive oil
1 tsp ground cumin
Pinch of cayenne
250g/9 oz large, cooked, peeled prawns, thawed
   completely if frozen
1 tbsp fresh lemon juice or wine vinegar
Freshly milled salt and black pepper

1. Finely chop or crush the garlic. Cut the potatoes into thick slices. Thinly slice the spring onions. Roughly chop some coriander and parsley to make about 2 tbsp of each. Crush the saffron (if using) lightly with the back of a spoon.

2. Put the oil, garlic, saffron, cumin and cayenne into a casserole, stir well, cover and cook on High for 1 minute.

3. Add the potatoes and 1 tbsp water, stirring until the potatoes are coated with the spice mixture. Cover and cook on High for about 5 minutes, stirring once, until just tender.

4. Stir in the prawns, lemon juice (or wine vinegar), spring onions and seasoning. Cover and cook on High for 2–3 minutes until hot throughout.

5. Adjust seasoning to taste if necessary and stir in the coriander and parsley gently before serving.

Pork Loin in Mustard Cream Sauce with Capers

Serve with buttered tagliatelle, freshly cooked rice or couscous with some chopped fresh parsley stirred in.

Serves 2

1 medium onion
1 garlic clove
2 fresh sage leaves
2 tbsp capers
350g/12 oz pork tenderloin
2 tsp olive oil
75ml/2½ fl oz dry white vermouth or wine
Freshly milled salt and black pepper
2 generous tsp wholegrain mustard
3 tbsp double cream

1. Thinly slice the onion. Finely chop the garlic and sage leaves. Rinse the capers and leave to drain. Cut the pork into thin slices.

2. Put the oil, onion, garlic and sage into a casserole. Cover and cook on High for 5 minutes, stirring once, until very soft.

3. Stir in the pork slices, cover and cook on High for 2 minutes.

4. Stir in the vermouth or wine and season lightly with salt and pepper. Cover and cook on High for 2 minutes.

5. Add the mustard and cream, stirring and pushing the pork into the liquid. Cover and cook on Medium for about 5 minutes or until the pork is cooked through and tender, stirring once.

6. Stir in half the capers and adjust the seasoning to taste. Serve scattered with the remaining capers.

Poussin with Walnut, Mushroom and Couscous Stuffing

An impressive and succulent dish – a whole stuffed chicken for one. We like to use free-range poussin for added flavour.

Serves 1

1 tbsp couscous
3 button mushrooms
4 walnut halves
Small bunch of flat-leaf parsley
2 tsp Worcestershire sauce
Freshly milled salt and black pepper
1 poussin
Oil for brushing
2 tbsp unsweetened orange juice

1. Put the kettle on to boil. Put the couscous into a bowl, pour over boiling water (from the kettle) to cover. Leave to stand, stirring occasionally. Finely chop the mushrooms, walnuts and parsley.
2. Drain the couscous in a sieve, pressing with the back of a spoon to extract as much water as possible and tip into a bowl. Stir in the Worcestershire sauce, mushrooms, walnuts and 1 tbsp of the chopped parsley. Season well.
3. Remove any ties from the poussin and with a sharp knife or scissors trim the ends of the legs, if necessary. Rinse the bird under running cold water and dry with kitchen paper inside and out. Loosen the skin over the breast by carefully working your fingers under it to form a pocket. Spoon the couscous stuffing into the pocket and press the skin over the stuffing.
4. Put the remaining chopped parsley onto a large plate. Brush the poussin all over with a little oil and roll it in the parsley until coated.
5. Put the poussin in a shallow dish, cover loosely, and cook on High for 14–16 minutes, or until cooked through (pierce the thickest part of the leg with a skewer, the juices should run clear). Lift the cooked poussin from the dish, cover and leave to stand for 5 minutes.
6. Meanwhile, stir the orange juice into the cooking juices and cook on High (no need to cover) for 2–3 minutes, stirring once until reduced a little.
7. Serve the poussin with the juices spooned over.

Chicken and Apricot Rolls

An impressive dish that is simplicity itself to make. For the best flavour choose free-range, organic or corn-fed chicken. Serve hot or cold with Italian style bread such as ciabatta and a crisp green salad tossed in oil-and-vinegar dressing. To serve one, simply halve the quantities and reduce the cooking time by about one third.

Serves 2

2 skinless, boneless chicken breasts
Freshly milled salt and black pepper
2 tsp ready-made mustard, such as Dijon
2 thin slices of good-quality ham
8 ready-to-eat dried apricots or stoned prunes

1. Put a chicken breast between two large pieces of clear film and bat with a rolling pin to make an even layer measuring slightly less than 1cm/½ inch thick. Repeat with the second chicken breast. Remove the top sheets of film.

2. Season the chicken breasts lightly with salt and pepper then spread 1 tsp mustard over each. Top with a slice of ham. Arrange 4 apricots along one short end of each.

3. Using the film to help you, roll the chicken up tightly from the same short end. Transfer the roll to a large square of non-stick baking paper and roll up, twisting the ends like a Christmas cracker to make a tight, evenly-shaped sausage. Repeat with the remaining chicken breast.

4. Place the parcels side by side in a shallow ovenproof dish, large enough to leave a space of 5–7.5cm/2–3 inches between them.

5. Cook on Medium for 15–20 minutes, turning the parcels (180°) once, or until cooked through. When a thin skewer is inserted through the paper and into the centre of the chicken, the juices should run clear.

6. Leave to stand for 5 minutes before unwrapping and cutting into thick slices. Serve with the juices spooned over the top. (To serve cold, leave the chicken in its wrapping and leave to cool completely before slicing.)

Venison with Chestnuts and Whisky

Whole, shelled, cooked chestnuts are available canned, frozen or in jars. Serve with rice, noodles or mashed potatoes.

Serves 2

2 shallots
1 garlic clove
Two 175g/6 oz venison steaks
2 tsp chicken bouillon powder
1 tbsp olive oil
2 tbsp whisky
1 tbsp plum sauce
6 cooked shelled chestnuts (see above)
4 fresh thyme sprigs
Freshly milled salt and black pepper

1. Put the kettle on to boil. Finely chop the shallots and garlic. Cut each venison steak into four slices. Dissolve the bouillon powder in a little hot water, about 2 tbsp.

2. Put the oil, garlic and shallots into a medium casserole, cover and cook on High for 3 minutes until softened.

3. Stir in the chicken stock, whisky, plum sauce, chestnuts and thyme sprigs. Cover and cook on High for 2 minutes, stirring once.

4. Put the venison into the casserole and turn the slices in the sauce until coated. Cover and cook on High for 2 minutes or until the venison is cooked. Season if necessary.

Simply
Sauces

The microwave is brilliant for cooking sauces; you can easily make small quantities and there are no sticky or burnt pans to wash up afterwards. Always use a deep container to allow plenty of room for the ingredients to boil up.

Our Really Useful Tomato Sauce recipe (see opposite) is great on pizza bases, in pasta, and in so many other ways, and our Really Useful White Sauce recipe (see page 88) is another versatile and indispensable basic sauce which can be put to use with savoury or sweet dishes. Both of the 'really useful' sauces are supplemented by a list of variations, each one adding different ingredients to the basic sauce so that you need never be at a loss for new flavours and new combinations.

Also in this section you will find three quick sauces for pasta (see page 89), and another three quick sauces, this time sweet ones (see page 89), which are perfect for puddings, both hot and cold.

Sauces are infinitely adaptable as accompaniments to grilled meat, grilled fish, jacket potatoes and a host of other meals and snacks. A good sauce can liven up a plain dish and transform it into something truly memorable.

Really Useful Tomato Sauce

A basic all-purpose tomato sauce that can be served in a myriad of ways – on pasta, vegetables, fish or chicken; or spread on wraps or pizza bases. It freezes and reheats well and there are lots of variations to choose from.

Serves 2–4, depending on how it is used

1 small onion
1 small carrot
1 small celery stick
1 garlic clove
400g can tomatoes, whole or chopped tomatoes
1 tbsp olive oil
150ml/¼ pint vegetable or chicken stock
2 tsp brown sugar
Freshly milled salt and black pepper

1. Chop the onion, carrot, celery and garlic very finely. If the tomatoes are whole, chop them up into their juices.
2. Put the oil, onion, carrot, celery and garlic into a casserole, cover and cook on High for 4 minutes until soft.
3. Stir in the tomatoes, stock, sugar and a little seasoning. Cover and cook on High for 8–10 minutes, stirring twice.
4. To make the sauce thicker (say for spreading on a pizza base), remove the cover and continue cooking on High until sufficiently reduced and thickened. To thin the sauce, add a little extra stock or water. Adjust the seasoning before serving.

Variations:
   Herb – stir a handful of chopped basil, parsley, rocket or watercress into the cooked sauce.
   Chilli – add chilli powder or chopped fresh chilli (see page 10) with the oil in step 2; add chilli sauce with the stock in step 3.
   Caper – add 1–2 tbsp chopped capers in step 3.
   Olive – add chopped green or black olives in step 3.
   Pesto – stir ready-made pesto into the cooked sauce.
   Sweetcorn – add drained canned sweetcorn in step 3.
   Anchovy – add few chopped anchovy fillets in step 2.
   Tuna – stir drained, canned tuna into the cooked sauce.
   Bacon – add 1–2 finely chopped bacon rashers in step 2.
   Ham, sausage – add chopped ham or cooked sausage (salami, chorizo or butchers) to the finished sauce.

Really Useful White Sauce

Another really simple sauce that can be easily adapted, depending on whether you are serving it with vegetables, fish or pasta; or as a sweet sauce with sponge puddings or cooked fruit. Stir frequently during cooking and you are guaranteed a smooth, lump-free sauce.

Serves 2–4, depending on how it is used

300ml/½ pint milk
15g/½ oz plain white flour or cornflour
15g/½ oz butter
Freshly milled salt and pepper

1. Put all the ingredients into a large jug or bowl (the sauce needs room to boil up). Cook (do not cover) on High for about 3 minutes, stirring frequently with a whisk, until the sauce thickens and comes to the boil.
2. Reduce the power to Medium-Low and continue cooking for a further 1–2 minutes.
3. Stir well and adjust the seasoning before serving.

Variations:
    Cream – replace half the milk with double cream.
    Cheese – stir in a handful of grated mature cheese (Cheddar, Parmesan) and ½ tsp mustard in step 3.
    Garlic Herb Cheese – crumble in some soft garlic-and-herb-flavoured cheese to the hot cooked sauce.
    Herb – add a handful of finely chopped parsley or mixed fresh herbs in step 3.
    Pesto – stir ready-made pesto into the cooked sauce.
    Salmon – stir flakes of cooked or canned salmon, or slivers of smoked salmon, into the cooked sauce.
    Prawn – add a handful of cooked, peeled prawns and a squeeze of lemon juice to the cooked sauce and heat until bubbling hot.
    Ham – stir some chopped ham into the cooked sauce.
    Sweet Vanilla – omit salt and pepper; add 1 tbsp sugar and a few drops of vanilla extract or paste.
    Boozy – omit salt and pepper, sweeten to taste with sugar or honey and stir in 2 tbsp brandy or rum.
    Chocolate – omit salt and pepper; stir a handful of grated chocolate into the hot cooked sauce.

Three Quick Sauces for Pasta

Each one serves 2, stirred into hot, cooked pasta.

Creamy Mushroom and Basil Sauce
Cook 100g/3½ oz sliced mushrooms, a crushed garlic clove and 15g/½ oz butter on High for 2–3 minutes until soft. Add 3 tbsp dry white vermouth or wine and cook on High for 1 minute until bubbling. Stir in 150ml/¼ pint double cream and cook on High for 2–3 minutes until thickened. Season to taste and stir in a handful of torn basil leaves.

Courgette and Lemon Sauce
Cook 2 grated courgettes with a crushed garlic clove and 25g/1 oz butter on High for 3 minutes until soft. Stir in 4 tbsp crème fraîche and 1 tbsp lemon juice and cook on High for 1 minute. Add a little finely grated lemon rind, chopped parsley, freshly grated Parmesan cheese and seasoning.

Red Pepper, Olive and Cheese Sauce
Cook 1 thinly sliced red onion with 1 thinly sliced red pepper and 2 tbsp olive oil in a covered casserole on High for 6–8 minutes, stirring once or twice, until soft. Stir in a small handful each of pitted black olives and basil leaves, 100g/3½ oz cubed cheese (a mixture of Cheddar and mozzarella) plus a little hot cooking water from the pasta.

Three Quick Sweet Sauces

Hot Raspberry Sauce
Good hot or cold with cheesecake, peaches or ice cream.
Cook 250g/9 oz crushed fresh raspberries with 3 tbsp redcurrant jelly on High for 1–2 minutes. Blend 1 tbsp cornflour with 2 tbsp cold water until smooth and stir into the fruit. Cook for 2–3 minutes, stirring often, until thickened and boiling. Add lemon juice to taste.

Cheat's Melba Sauce
Serve warm with ice cream or fresh fruit such as peaches.
Heat 4 tbsp each of raspberry jam and redcurrant jelly, with 2 tbsp lemon juice on High for 1–2 minutes. Stir well until melted.

Butterscotch Sauce
Delicious with sponge puddings, desserts made with bananas, or spooned over ice cream. Serve warm.
Cook 50g/1¾ oz each of butter and soft brown sugar with 175g/6 oz golden syrup on High for about 2 minutes, stirring once. Stir well until blended, add 2 tsp lemon juice and 150ml/¼ pint double cream. Cook on High for ½-1 minute until just bubbling.

Family Eats

10

Here is a repertoire of family favourites, a collection of instantly appealing, flavourful dishes, substantial enough to satisfy the most demanding appetites, and quick to prepare. Some of them can be rustled up in a mere 15 minutes – so the pressure is relieved if you've arrived home late to find a pent-up demand for dinner to be served.

Here you will find a dish to suit every day of the week and every occasion. A rice dish like Jambalaya (see page 96), can be ready in just 30 minutes.

There are fragrant overtones to be found in Scented Lamb with Rosemary and Apricots (see page 99) and Lamb and Aubergine with Minted Yogurt (see page 100). For other savoury treats, try Vegetables in Creamy Pesto Sauce with Crispy Bacon (see page 94) or Cheat's Pizza (see opposite), a variation on the classic Italian dish which has a large naan bread replacing the usual pizza base.

Cheat's Pizza

Easily adapted to serve one, two or more, and the topping can be customised to suit individuals. Serve with lots of salad. Look out for jars of pimientos, Spanish sweet peppers, roasted and preserved in oil.

Serves 4, or 2 larger appetites

1 onion
1 garlic clove
8 button mushrooms
1 red pimiento, drained
55g/2 oz mozzarella cheese
100g/3½ oz mature Cheddar cheese
2 tbsp olive oil
150ml/¼ pint passata
Freshly milled salt and black pepper
2 large plain naan breads
Small handful of spinach leaves
Handful of stoned black olives (optional)
A few fresh oregano leaves
1 tsp pine nuts

1. Thinly slice the onion and crush the garlic. Chop the mushrooms and thinly slice the pimiento. Tear the mozzarella cheese into small pieces and coarsely grate the Cheddar cheese.
2. Put the onion, garlic and 1 tbsp of the oil in a casserole. Cover and cook on High for 3 minutes until softened. Stir in the mushrooms, passata and a little seasoning.
3. Put the naan breads onto individual large flat plates. Spread some of the mushroom mixture over the top of each one. Top with the spinach leaves, pimiento pieces and the two cheeses. Scatter over the olives (if using), oregano leaves, pine nuts and remaining oil.
4. Cook, one at a time, on High (no need to cover) for about 4 minutes until piping hot and the cheese has melted. Cut into portions and serve immediately.

Variations:
Replace the mushrooms, spinach leaves and pimiento with:
*   A drained 200g can tuna, 55g/2 oz sweetcorn and a few anchovy pieces.
*   6 slices of salami (quartered), a small handful of rocket leaves and wedges of canned artichoke hearts.
*   Roasted vegetables, diced, smoked ham and a few raisins.

Sweet and Sour Vegetables

To serve this with rice, either cook the rice first (see page 103) and reheat it just before serving, or cook the vegetables and let them stand while the rice is in the microwave.

Serves 4

Selection of vegetables, such as:
1 medium onion
1 garlic clove
2 celery sticks
2 medium carrots
200g/7 oz cauliflower
100g/3½ oz chestnut mushrooms
75g/2¾ oz mange-touts
1 red pepper

400g can whole plum tomatoes
3 tbsp dark brown sugar
2 tsp cornflour
2 tbsp wine vinegar
2 tbsp soy sauce
2 tsp oil
Freshly milled salt and black pepper

1. Finely chop the onion and garlic. Thinly slice the celery. Thickly slice the carrots. Cut the cauliflower into small florets. Quarter the mushrooms. Thickly slice the mange-touts. Halve the red pepper, remove and discard the seeds and stalk, and slice thinly.
2. Tip the tomatoes into a sieve and, with your hand, break them up into pieces, allowing the liquid to drain away. Transfer the tomatoes to a bowl or jug and stir in the sugar, cornflour, vinegar and soy sauce.
3. Put the oil, onion and garlic into a large casserole, cover and cook on High for 3 minutes until softened.
4. Stir in the celery and carrots, cover and cook on High for 3 minutes.
5. Mix in the cauliflower, mange-touts, red pepper and mushrooms. Cover and cook on High for 3 minutes.
6. Add the tomato mixture, stirring until the vegetables are coated. Cover and cook on High for about 5 minutes, stirring once, or until the sauce has thickened and the vegetables are cooked to your liking.
7. Season to taste. Cover and leave to stand for a few minutes before serving.

Rainbow Vegetables with Gammon

Using different-coloured vegetables not only looks bright on the plate but is also really healthy. Serve with rice or noodles.

Serves 4

1 medium red onion
Small piece of fresh root ginger
2 garlic cloves
4 spring onions
2 large carrots
2 large courgettes
2 pak choi
2 gammon steaks
2 tsp olive oil
1 tbsp vegetable bouillon powder
2 tbsp sweet chilli sauce
2 tbsp wholegrain mustard
Freshly milled black pepper

1. Put the kettle on to boil. Very thinly slice the onion, ginger and garlic. Cut the spring onions, carrots and courgettes into very thin strips. Finely shred the pak choi. Remove any fat from the gammon and cut into bite-size pieces.

2. Put the oil, onion, ginger, garlic and carrots into a casserole, cover and cook on High for 2 minutes.

3. Stir in the gammon pieces, cover and cook on High for 3 minutes, stirring once.

4. Pour 150ml/¼ pint boiling water (from the kettle) into a jug and stir in the bouillon powder, chilli sauce, wholegrain mustard and a little black pepper.

5. Stir the courgettes and spring onions into the casserole and pour the stock mixture over.

6. Cover and cook on High for about 6 minutes, stirring twice until piping hot and the gammon is cooked. Stir in the pak choi and cook a further minute.

Vegetables in Creamy Pesto Sauce with Crispy Bacon

Change the vegetables to suit the seasons and your family's preferred choices. Vary it too by adding cooked chicken pieces or diced ham in step 6.

Serves 4

2 medium onions
2 medium carrots
1 garlic clove
1–2 sweet potatoes, total weight about 675g/1½ lb
175g/6 oz chestnut mushrooms
1 generous tbsp pesto
100ml/3½ fl oz single cream
8 thin rindless streaky bacon rashers
100g/3½ oz frozen peas
100g/3½ oz frozen sweetcorn
Freshly milled salt and black pepper

1. Thinly slice the onions and carrots. Crush the garlic. Cut the sweet potatoes into small even-size cubes. Thickly slice the mushrooms. Stir the pesto into the cream. Cut the bacon into thin strips.
2. Put the onions and garlic into a large casserole, cover and cook on High for 3 minutes until just soft.
3. Stir in the carrots, sweet potatoes and 2 tbsp water. Cover and cook on High for 8 minutes, stirring once or twice.
4. Add the mushrooms, peas and sweetcorn, cover and cook on High for a further 5 minutes until the vegetables are just tender. Leave to stand, covered, while you cook the bacon.
5. Put the bacon into a wide ovenproof dish and cook on High for 5–8 minutes, stirring occasionally and pouring off excess fat, until lightly browned and crisp. Drain on kitchen paper.
6. Stir the cream mixture into the hot vegetables, cover and cook on High for about 2 minutes until hot throughout. Season if necessary.
7. Serve the vegetables and sauce with the crisp bacon sprinkled over.

Mediterranean Fish Fillets

Succulent fish sits on a bed of lemon-scented spinach and leeks. You can use lemon juice in place of the lemon myrtle.

Serves 4

1 leek
6 medium-size Italian tomatoes
Bunch of watercress
Small bunch of fresh fennel leaves
Small bunch of fresh parsley
500g/1 lb 2 oz skinless fish fillet, such as salmon, plaice or trout
1 tbsp fish or vegetable bouillon powder
2 tsp lemon myrtle
2 tbsp tomato purée
Freshly milled black pepper
A large handful of small spinach leaves

1. Finely chop the leek and roughly chop the tomatoes. Pull the watercress leaves off the stalks. Finely chop the fennel and parsley. Cut the fish fillet into four portions.

2. Pour 4 tbsp water into a wide casserole and stir in the bouillon powder, lemon myrtle, tomato purée and a little black pepper. Mix in the chopped leek and tomatoes, cover and cook on High for 5 minutes until the leeks have softened.

3. Stir in the watercress and spinach leaves and space the fish portions evenly around the edge of the dish. Sprinkle the chopped herbs over the fish and spinach.

4. Cover and cook on High for 3 minutes or until the fish is just cooked.

Jambalaya

Vary the flavour by adding some cooked, peeled prawns or thin slices of spicy sausage, such as chorizo, for the final 5 minutes of cooking.

Serves 4–6

2 medium onions
2 celery sticks
2 garlic cloves
1 red pepper
1 medium courgette
4 spring onions
500g/1 lb 2 oz skinless, boneless chicken, such as thigh, breast or a mixture
2 tbsp olive oil
1 chicken stock cube
1 tsp sweet chilli sauce
150g/5½ oz easy-cook long grain rice
1 tbsp tomato purée
Good pinch of cayenne
Freshly milled salt and black pepper
Small handful of fresh parsley leaves, the flat-leaf variety if possible

1.   Finely chop the onions, celery and garlic. Halve the red pepper, remove and discard the seeds and stalk, and chop into small pieces. Chop the courgette. Thinly slice the spring onions. Cut the chicken into small bite-size pieces. Put the kettle on to boil.

2.   Put the oil into a large casserole with the onions, celery and garlic. Cover and cook on High for 5 minutes until soft.

3.   Dissolve the stock cube in 500ml/18 fl oz boiling water (from the kettle) and stir into the onion mixture with the chicken and chilli sauce. Cover and cook on High for 5 minutes.

4.   Stir in the rice, red pepper, courgette, tomato purée and cayenne. Cook (no need to cover) on High for about 20 minutes, stirring occasionally until the rice and vegetables are cooked and almost all the liquid has been absorbed.

5.   Season to taste and stir in some parsley. Cover and leave to stand for a few minutes before serving with the spring onions scattered over the top.

Chicken Meatballs with Pepper and Peanut Sauce

We've made these meatballs with chicken but they are equally delicious made with minced turkey, beef or venison. If you have the time, buy pieces of meat and whizz into mince with a food processor. Serve with noodles or new potatoes.

Serves 4

1 onion
1 garlic clove
1 lime
2 red peppers
Small bunch of fresh coriander
500g/1 lb 2 oz minced chicken
1 medium egg
Freshly milled salt and black pepper
1 tbsp plain flour
2 tsp vegetable oil
2 tbsp smooth peanut butter
1 tbsp chicken bouillon powder

1. Put the kettle on to boil. Finely chop the onion and crush the garlic. Grate the rind from the lime, cut in half and squeeze out the juice. Cut the peppers in half, remove and discard the seeds and stalks, and chop finely. Finely chop the coriander.

2. Put the minced chicken into a bowl and with a fork mix in the egg, chopped coriander, lime rind and juice and a little seasoning. With damp hands shape the mixture into 20 meatballs and dust with the flour.

3. Put the oil, chopped onion, garlic and meatballs in a large casserole. Cook (no need to cover) on High for 5 minutes, rearranging the meatballs half way through cooking.

4. Spoon the peanut butter and bouillon powder into a jug and whisk in 150ml/¼ pint boiling water (from the kettle). Stir in the chopped peppers and pour the mixture over and around the meatballs.

5. Cover and cook on Medium for 4 minutes, stirring once or twice, or until the meatballs are cooked through. Season the sauce if necessary before serving.

Chicken and Coconut Curry

We like to serve this with naan bread to mop up the creamy sauce. Alternatively, leave the cooked curry to stand (covered) while you cook some basmati rice (see method for cooking rice on page 103). Chicken thighs give the best flavour, though chicken breast is delicious too.

Serves 5–6

1 medium onion
1 garlic clove
1 small lemon
1kg/2¼ lb boneless chicken (breast, thighs or a mixture)
2 tsp oil
2 tbsp curry powder
1 tbsp plain flour
1 chicken stock cube
400ml can coconut milk
Freshly milled salt and black pepper
Small handful of fresh coriander leaves

1. Finely chop the onion and garlic. Finely grate the rind from the lemon and squeeze out 1 tbsp juice. Cut the chicken into bite-size pieces. Put the kettle on to boil.

2. Put the oil, onion and garlic into a casserole, cover and cook on High for 3 minutes until softened.

3. Stir in the chicken, curry powder, flour and lemon rind. Cover and cook on High for 6 minutes.

4. Meanwhile, dissolve the stock cube in 100ml/3½ fl oz boiling water (from the kettle). Stir the stock into the chicken, cover and cook on High for 6 minutes.

5. Add 1 tbsp lemon juice and the coconut milk. Cook (no need to cover) on High for about 5 minutes or until the sauce is bubbling hot and the chicken is cooked through.

6. Season to taste. Serve with the coriander leaves scattered over the top.

Scented Lamb with Rosemary and Apricots

Vary the flavour by replacing the apricots and rosemary with stoned prunes and sprigs of mint. This recipe is also delicious when made with diced chicken. Serve with rice, noodles or piled onto jacket potatoes.

Serves 4

2 onions
8 dried apricots
500g/1 lb 2 oz lean lamb
1 tbsp vegetable oil
1 tbsp plain flour
2 tbsp sesame seeds
1 tbsp lamb bouillon powder
2 sprigs fresh rosemary
175g/6 oz frozen peas
Freshly milled salt and black pepper

1. Put the kettle on to boil. Finely chop the onions. Cut the apricots into narrow strips. Trim any excess fat from the lamb and cut into bite-size pieces.

2. Put the onions and oil into a large casserole. Cover and cook on High for 5 minutes until softened.

3. Stir in the pieces of lamb, flour and sesame seeds. Cover and cook on High for 5 minutes, stirring once.

4. Sprinkle over the bouillon powder, 150ml/¼ pint boiling water (from the kettle), apricot pieces and rosemary sprigs and stir until thoroughly mixed.

5. Cover and cook on Medium for 15 minutes, stirring twice, until the lamb is tender.

6. Stir in the peas, cover and cook on Medium for 5 minutes. Season if necessary before serving.

Lamb and Aubergine with Minted Yogurt

We like to serve this in warmed bowls with fresh crusty bread for mopping up the juices. The flavour of allspice resembles a mixture of cloves, cinnamon and nutmeg, and goes particularly well with lamb.

Serves 4

1 large onion
1 medium carrot
1 celery stick
2 garlic cloves
1 small-to-medium aubergine
1 tsp olive oil
500g/1 lb 2 oz lean minced lamb
400g can chopped tomatoes
1 generous tsp ground allspice
1 generous tsp vegetable bouillon powder
Freshly milled salt and black pepper
Small handful of fresh mint leaves
1 tsp sugar
150ml/¼ pint natural yogurt, preferably Greek style

1. Finely chop the onion, carrot, celery and garlic. Cut the aubergine into cubes measuring about 1cm/½ inch. Put the kettle on to boil.
2. Put the chopped onion, carrot, celery, garlic and oil into a large casserole. Cover and cook on High for 5 minutes until softened.
3. Stir in the lamb, aubergine, tomatoes, allspice and bouillon powder. Season lightly with salt and pepper. Add 150ml/¼ pint boiling water (from the kettle), stirring until well mixed. Cover and cook on High for 15 minutes, stirring occasionally, or until the aubergine is soft and the lamb is cooked.
4. Meanwhile, finely chop the mint leaves with the sugar. Stir the mint-sugar mixture into the yogurt, cover and leave to stand.
5. When the lamb mixture is cooked, either serve it immediately or, if time allows, continue cooking on Medium for a further 10 minutes – this develops the flavour even further.
6. Serve the lamb and aubergine topped with a generous spoonful of minted yogurt.

Fast Toppings & Sidelines

11

So much interest can be added to a meal by a well judged extra. Sidelines and fast toppings provide a perfect contrast and complement to a main dish, and they are quick and easy to run up in the microwave.

You may not have thought of using your microwave to make a snappy poppadom (see page 103) to go with your curry, or a warm bread roll (see overleaf) to go with your soup, but they both work a treat.

Toppings such as crisp croûtons (see overleaf), crispy bacon (see page 103), golden onions (see page 103), toasted coconut (see page 104) or toasted almonds and pine nuts (see page 104) are all microwave successes; they add crunchiness and a last-minute flourish to savoury or sweet dishes. Spiced nuts (see page 104) are great to serve with drinks.

Sidelines add savour and substance to your meals. Fast toppings add flavour and texture and a touch of flair.

A Warm Bread Roll

Sometimes a warm bread roll is just what is needed to accompany a simple bowl of soup or vegetables.

Just sit them on a plate and heat through (no need to cover) on Medium until just warm to the touch, taking care not to overheat. Heating times will depend on the type and size of the bread rolls. Expect one or two rolls to take about 30 seconds, three or four rolls up to 1 minute.

Crisp Croûtons

For adding crunch to soups and salads.

Brush some bread slices with oil or spread them with soft butter (plain or with a little crushed garlic stirred in). Trim off the crusts and cut the bread into small even-size cubes. Spread them, in a single layer, on an ovenproof plate and cook (do not cover) on Medium-High until golden brown. Watch them carefully and stir often to prevent them from catching and burning. Expect cubes from one bread slice to take 1–2 minutes, two slices about 3 minutes. They will continue crisping as they cool.

Crunchy Breadcrumbs

Ideal for topping vegetable dishes and anything served in a sauce.

Spread fresh breadcrumbs in an even layer on an ovenproof plate or shallow dish and cook (do not cover) on Medium or Medium-High until dry and golden brown. Watch them carefully, stirring frequently, to make sure they do not catch and burn. 50–100g/1¾–3½ oz breadcrumbs should take about 3–4 minutes.

Buttery Crumbs

Lovely as a topping for vegetables and salads, particularly when some finely chopped parsley and finely grated lemon rind is mixed with the buttery crumbs. Stir in some demerara sugar and you have a crunchy topping for ice cream, fruit and other puddings.

Melt 25g/1 oz butter in a shallow ovenproof dish (30–40 seconds on High) and stir in about 50g/1¾ oz fresh breadcrumbs. Cook (do not cover) on Medium or Medium-High for 2–3 minutes or until crisp and golden brown. Watch them carefully, stirring often to prevent them burning. They will continue crisping as they cool.

Crispy Bacon

Lovely sprinkled over eggs, vegetables, soups and salads.

Follow the method on page 94, step 5.

Golden Onions

Crisp golden strips of onion are delicious scattered on vegetables, salads and dishes made with rice or grains.

Thinly slice an onion and put it into a small casserole with 2 tsp oil and a generous pinch of sugar, stirring well. Cook (do not cover) on High, stirring occasionally, until golden brown. Expect one small onion to take about 5 minutes.

Snappy Poppadoms

The perfect accompaniment to curries and other spicy dishes.

Best results come when cooking two at a time. Leave them plain or brush one side of each poppadom lightly with oil and cook (one on top of the other with no cover) on High for about 1 minute until puffed up and crisp.

A Bowl of Rice

Cooking rice in the microwave may take as long as it would on the hob, but it is very convenient. Use this method for long-grain, basmati and fragrant rice.

For 1–2 servings, put 100g/3½ oz white rice into a large bowl or casserole and stir in 450ml/16 fl oz boiling water from the kettle (750ml/1¼ pints for brown rice). Cook (do not cover) on High for about 10 minutes (about 20 minutes for brown rice). There is normally no need to stir the rice during cooking. At the end of cooking, the rice may still retain a 'bite' with some liquid still remaining in the bowl. Simply cover and leave to stand for 5 minutes during which time the rice will finish softening and the liquid will be absorbed. Fluff up the rice with a fork before serving.

Toasted Coconut

Lovely for topping a bowl of ice cream.

Spread desiccated coconut in a even layer on an ovenproof plate. Cook (do not cover) on Medium-High until golden brown. Watch it carefully, stirring a few times, to make sure it does not catch and burn. Expect 100g/3½ oz to take about 3–4 minutes, 200g/7 oz 5–6 minutes.

Toasted Nuts

Almonds (whole, chopped or flaked) and pine nuts are particularly good toasted in the microwave. Scatter them over savoury or sweet dishes to add their unique flavour and texture.

Spread the nuts in an even layer (a single layer if possible) on an ovenproof plate and cook (do not cover) on Medium-High until lightly and evenly browned. 100g/3½ oz are likely to take 4–5 minutes.

Spiced Nuts

Tasty appetiser to serve with drinks. And you could vary the flavours – try using just one type of nut, or replacing the spices with curry powder.

Put 250g/9 oz mixed nuts in a shallow ovenproof dish, stir in 2 tsp oil and cook (do not cover) on Medium-High for 1½ minutes. Mix 1–2 tsp chilli power with 1 tsp ground cumin, ½ tsp ground coriander and a generous pinch of salt and stir into the nuts. Continue cooking (do not cover) on Medium-High for 2–3 minutes. With a slotted spoon, lift out and drain on kitchen paper before leaving to cool.

Puds in a Flash

12

Your microwave does puddings to perfection. For some self-indulgent luxury to round off dinner, or at any time of the day, this cornucopia of sweet-toothed treats shows just what a range your microwave can offer you. Rest assured, the results will be amazing.

A microwave cooks fruit beautifully, and will do wonders with Hot Sticky Figs (see overleaf) and Plums in Rich Red Wine Syrup (see page 107). Sponge puddings, such as the Banana, Almond and Honey Pudding (see page 109) will amaze and delight, as too will puddings containing eggs, like the Cherry and Hazelnut Brioche Pudding (see page 110) so long as Low/Medium power is used. We know the American-style Upside-down Cheesecake (see page 111) goes down a treat.

Chocolate is so easy to melt in the microwave. The mouth-watering individual portions of Soft Chocolate and Fresh Orange Pots (see page 108) are stylishly served in small dishes or ramekins.

Hot Sticky Figs

Spectacularly simple with the luxurious flavours of maple syrup, almond biscuits and liqueur. Let your guests open the parcels at the table. An easy recipe to adapt for extra guests. You will need two squares of greaseproof paper, twice the size of each fig.

Serves 2

1 small orange
3 amaretti biscuits
2 tbsp maple syrup
1 tbsp amaretto liqueur
3 tbsp double cream
2 large fresh figs

1.   Grate the rind from half the orange, cut in half and squeeze the juice. Crush the biscuits.

2.   Pour the maple syrup into a small bowl and stir in the, crushed biscuits, amaretto liqueur, half of the grated orange rind and all of the orange juice.

3.   Spoon the cream into a small dish and stir in ¼ tsp of the remaining grated orange rind.

4.   Cut a cross through each fig, from the top almost to the base (and making sure you don't cut right through), and open out.

5.   Place each fig in the centre of a square of greaseproof paper. Spoon some of the biscuit mixture into the centre of the figs. Gather the four corners of the paper and twist until secured, making two parcels.

6.   Lift the fig parcels onto a shallow dish and cook on High (no need to cover) for 2 minutes. Serve in the paper with the orange-flavoured cream.

Plums in Rich Red Wine Syrup

Cooking on Medium power for part of the time helps to retain the shape of the plums. Serve them hot, warm or chilled in the deep red syrup with its subtle hint of spices. Vanilla ice cream or a spoonful of thick (maybe clotted) cream goes well alongside.

Serves 4

500g/1 lb 2 oz red plums
3 tbsp caster sugar
1 star anise
1 small cinnamon stick
150ml/¼ pint red wine
Crisp biscuits, to serve

1. Halve the plums, removing and discarding the stones. Put the plum halves in an even layer in a casserole. Sprinkle the sugar over the top and tuck the star anise and cinnamon stick between them. Pour the red wine over the top.

2. Cover and cook on High for 5 minutes, then lower the microwave power to Medium and cook for a further 5 minutes or until the plums are soft but still retain their shape.

3. Cover and leave to stand for 10 minutes or more before serving.

Soft Chocolate and Fresh Orange Pots

The rich chocolate mixture hides a refreshing surprise – pieces of fresh orange segment. For serious chocoholics, omit the orange segments and, instead, serve them alongside the pots of chocolate, or indeed not at all!

Serves 4

150ml/¼ pint double cream
5 tbsp milk
1 small orange
25g/1 oz icing sugar
1 large egg yolk
100g/3½ oz dark chocolate with about 70% cocoa solids

1. Put the cream and milk into a heatproof jug. Finely grate about ½ tsp rind from the orange and stir into the cream mixture.

2. With a sharp knife, cut off the rind and pith from the orange and, running the knife between the segment divisions, cut out the orange flesh (there should be no skin attached). Cut each segment into two or three pieces and divide them between four small dishes or ramekins.

3. Whisk the sugar and egg yolk until pale and thick (easiest done with an electric hand whisk).

4. Break the chocolate into a bowl and heat on Medium for 3–4 minutes, stirring once, until melted.

5. Heat the cream mixture on High for about 2 minutes or until just boiling.

6. Add the melted chocolate and the hot milk to the egg mixture and beat until well mixed, smooth and shiny. Pour over the orange segments in the dishes.

7. Leave to cool then refrigerate for several hours or over-night before serving.

Banana, Almond and Honey Pudding

Serve this delicate pudding with a good, thick Greek-style yogurt. For a really good flavour, make sure you use a banana that is ripe. In place of honey, you could try using maple syrup or golden syrup for an alternative flavour.

Serves 6

125g/4½ oz soft butter, plus extra for greasing
2–3 tbsp clear honey
1 generous tbsp flaked almonds
125g/4½ oz caster sugar
2 medium eggs
2 tbsp milk
100g/3½ oz self-raising flour
25g/1 oz ground almonds
1 tsp baking powder
1 medium banana

1. Butter a 1.2 litre/2 pint pudding bowl and press a small disc of baking paper in the bottom. Spoon the honey onto the paper and scatter the flaked almonds on top.

2. Put the butter into a large mixing bowl and add the sugar, eggs and milk. Sift the flour, ground almonds and baking powder over the top. With a hand-held mixer or a wooden spoon, beat the mixture until light and smooth.

3. Peel and mash the banana and quickly stir it into the pudding mixture. Spoon the mixture into the prepared pudding bowl. Place a square of baking paper over the top and, with your hands, crimp it down the sides of the bowl to form a loose 'hat'.

4. Cook on Medium-High for 6–8 minutes until just cooked through (a wooden cocktail stick inserted in the centre should come out clean). Take care not to overcook it.

5. Leave to stand for a few minutes before carefully running a knife around the sides, turning the pudding out onto a warmed serving plate and removing the disc of paper.

Cherry and Hazelnut Brioche Pudding

A twist on the classic bread and butter pudding. Brioche is a rich bread which gives a lighter pudding, while hazelnuts and cherries add style. Remember there is a 'soaking time' of 30 minutes. Serve with custard, cream or natural yogurt.

Serves 4

55g/2 oz butter, plus extra for greasing
200g/7 oz stoned cherries, thawed if frozen
100g/3½ oz toasted hazelnuts
6 thin slices of brioche bread, about 175g/6 oz
2 tbsp soft brown sugar
300ml/½ pint milk
3 medium eggs
1 tsp vanilla extract
Icing sugar, for sifting

1. Butter a 1.2 litre/2 pint pudding bowl and press a small disc of baking paper in the bottom. Roughly chop the cherries and hazelnuts.

2. Butter one side of the brioche slices. Over three of the slices, scatter some brown sugar, chopped cherries and hazelnuts. Make 'sandwiches' by topping each with the remaining buttered slices and cut each into four.

3. Layer the sandwiches in the bowl and press down gently.

4. Put the milk into a jug and mix in the eggs and vanilla extract.

5. Pour the milk mixture through a sieve over the 'sandwiches' and leave for at least 30 minutes for the liquid to be absorbed.

6. Cook (no need to cover) on Medium for about 14 minutes until set. Serve from the bowl or turn onto a plate and sift over a little icing sugar.

Upside-down Cheesecake

Cooked upside down to make sure the biscuit base retains its crispness, then served the right way up! Serve just as it is or topped with some fresh summer fruit, such as raspberries.

Serves 8

Butter for greasing
3 medium eggs
1 small lemon
2 tbsp cornflour
125g/4½ oz caster sugar
250g/9 oz soft curd cheese
250g/9 oz quark
½ tsp vanilla extract
140g/5 oz chocolate biscuits (covered with chocolate on one side only)

1. Butter a cake dish measuring 20cm/8 inches in diameter and 5cm/2 inches deep. Line the base and sides with non-stick baking paper, making sure the paper on the sides stands 5cm/2 inches above the top of the dish.
2. Separate the eggs, putting the whites into one mixing bowl and the yolks into another. Finely grate the rind from the lemon, halve it and squeeze out the juice. Mix the cornflour with the sugar and stir into the egg yolks. Add the curd cheese, quark, vanilla, lemon rind and juice. Using an electric hand mixer or wooden spoon, beat well until smooth.
3. With clean beaters, whisk the egg whites until stiff peaks form. With a large metal spoon, fold one third of the egg foam into the cheese mixture, then fold in the remainder. Tip into the prepared dish and level the surface.
4. Cook on Medium for about 20 minutes until set. Leave to stand for 5 minutes.
5. Break the biscuits into a food processor and whizz to make very fine crumbs. Tip the crumbs on top of the hot cheesecake and, with the back of a spoon, gently spread them evenly over the surface. Cook on Medium for about 2 minutes to melt the chocolate.
6. Leave to cool then refrigerate for several hours or overnight.
7. With scissors, cut the paper collar down to the top of the biscuits and carefully turn the cheesecake out onto a serving plate. Peel off the remaining paper and serve.

Coffee Meringue Cream with Mango and Blueberries

A very indulgent pudding.

Serves 2

1 mango
1 tbsp instant espresso coffee
2 meringue baskets, about 55g/2 oz
150ml/¼ pint double cream
200g/7 oz blueberries
1 tbsp rum (optional)
3 tbsp natural yogurt
2 tbsp demerara sugar

1. Put the kettle on to boil. Peel the mango and cut the flesh away from the stone, then thinly slice the flesh. Tip the coffee into a cup and dissolve in a tablespoon of hot water (from the kettle). Roughly crush the meringues. Lightly whip the cream.

2. Spoon the mango slices and blueberries into two individual dishes and drizzle over the rum, if using. Cook on High (no need to cover) for 3 minutes.

3. Meanwhile, stir the yogurt, crushed meringue and coffee into the whipped cream.

4. Spoon the creamy mixture over the hot fruits and sprinkle over the sugar. Cook (no need to cover) on Medium for 3 minutes until heated through. Serve immediately.

Spiced Apples with Almond Custard

*An almond-flavoured custard smothers spicy apples and sul-
tanas. Crushed macaroon biscuits add a crisp topping.*

Serves 4–6

Butter, for greasing
4 eating apples
1 orange
4 macaroon biscuits
1 tsp ground mixed spice
150ml/¼ pint unsweetened apple juice
1 tsp vanilla extract
100g/3½ oz sultanas
½ tsp cornflour
300ml/½ pint milk
3 medium eggs
2 tbsp soft brown sugar
55g/2 oz ground almonds

1. Butter a 20cm/8 inch cake dish. Peel and core the apples
    and slice thinly. Finely grate the orange rind, cut in half
    and squeeze the juice. Crush the macaroon biscuits.

2. In a jug, mix together the orange rind and juice, mixed
    spice, apple juice and vanilla extract.

3. Spread the apple slices over the bottom of the buttered
    dish. Scatter over the sultanas and drizzle over the orange
    mixture. Cook (no need to cover) on High for 3 minutes.

4. Blend the cornflour to a smooth paste with a little of the
    milk and stir in the eggs, beating until well mixed.

5. Pour the remaining milk into a large jug, cover and cook
    on High for 3 minutes. Whisk the hot milk into the egg
    mixture, pour back into the jug, cover loosely and cook on
    High for 1 minute until thickened like custard.

6. Stir the brown sugar and almonds into the custard and
    pour over the apple mixture. Sprinkle over the crushed
    macaroons. Cover loosely and cook on High for 1 minute.
    Serve hot or cold.

Dark Chocolate Fondue

A luxurious dessert or an indulgent treat for any time that chocolate feeling comes over you! It is also ideal for serving as a sauce spooned over ice cream, fruit and other desserts. It reheats well too – use Medium power and stir frequently.

Serves 2

100g/3½ oz good-quality dark chocolate with about 70% solids
2 tsp clear honey
5 tbsp double cream
1 tsp vanilla extract
2–3 tsp brandy or rum (optional)
Crisp biscuits, sponge fingers, dried fruit (apricots, dates) and fresh fruit (orange segments, pear slices, pineapple chunks), to serve

1. Break the chocolate into squares and put into a bowl. Add the honey and cream.

2. Heat on Medium-High (no need to cover) for 1½–2 minutes, stirring at least twice, or until the chocolate has melted and the mixture becomes smooth and glossy.

3. Stir in the vanilla extract and the brandy or rum, if using.

4. Serve immediately with biscuits, sponge fingers and fruit for dipping.

Cakes & Preserves 13

Why not make cakes in your microwave? Don't expect them to look and feel like cakes that have been baked in the traditional way – there is, for example, no surface browning or crisping, so they will need to be eaten up quickly. Distinctive and unusual they may be, they are fun to make and we really like the results.

We have chosen recipes based on processes and ingredients which a microwave deals with very well, such as Iced Orange Gingerbread (see overleaf) which is made by melting the fat and sugar together, Apple and Saffron Cake (see page 117), a moist cake containing fresh fruit, and the shortbread-style mixture needed for Blueberry Shortcake (see page 118).

Home-made preserves are always a special treat, but how often do you end up making far more than you need? Microwaves are ideal for cooking up small quantities of jam, marmalade, fruit butters, curds and chutney. The colours are so bright and the flavours are so fresh. You can take advantage of small quantities of fruit or other ingredients that happen to be in season or growing in your own garden.

Always use a container that can withstand the extreme heat of boiling sugar; make sure it is very large, allowing plenty of room for the ingredients to boil up, and for evaporation.

And don't forget, preserves make lovely gifts, especially when they are this good.

Iced Orange Gingerbread

This cake has a close texture and rich flavour that is offset by the sweet icing – perfect with a cup of strong coffee.

Serves 6–8

55g/2 oz butter, plus extra for greasing
200g/7 oz plain flour
1 tsp baking powder
2 tsp ground ginger
Pinch of salt
1 medium egg
100ml/3½ fl oz milk
1 small orange
85g/3 oz soft dark brown sugar
100g/3½ oz golden syrup
150g/5½ oz icing sugar

1. Butter a cake dish measuring 20cm/8 inches in diameter and 5cm/2 inches deep. Line the base with a circle of non-stick baking paper.
2. Into a mixing bowl, sift the flour, baking powder, ginger and salt. Break the egg into a bowl, beat lightly with a fork and stir in the milk. Finely grate the rind from half the orange.
3. Put the butter, brown sugar and syrup into a heatproof jug and cook on High for about 1 minute until the butter has melted. Stir well to dissolve the sugar.
4. Add the syrup and milk mixtures to the flour and beat well until smooth. Pour into the prepared dish.
5. Cook (do not cover) on Medium-High for 7–8 minutes or until just cooked in the centre and still slightly moist on the surface (a wooden cocktail stick inserted in the centre should come out clean).
6. Leave the cake to stand in its dish for 5 minutes before carefully running a knife round the sides and turning it out onto a cooling rack, removing the lining paper as you do so. Leave to cool.
7. Meanwhile, halve the orange and squeeze out 2 tbsp juice. Sift the icing sugar and stir in the orange juice to make a smooth icing. Pour over the top of the cake and down the sides. Leave to set before serving.

Apple and Saffron Cake

Saffron gives the cake its pretty yellow colour and delicate, distinctive flavour. Serve it warm as a dessert or at room temperature with a cup of tea or coffee. A spoonful of thick cream or crème fraîche goes well with it.

Serves 6–8

Pinch of saffron threads
100g/3½ oz soft butter, plus extra for greasing
2 medium eggs
125g/4½ oz plain flour
1 tsp baking powder
½ tsp ground mixed spice
2 medium eating apples, total weight about 225g/8 oz
125g/4½ oz caster sugar
1 tbsp milk or apple juice
Icing sugar, for sifting over

1. Put the saffron into a small bowl, crush lightly with the back of a small spoon and stir in 1 tbsp water. Heat on High for 15 seconds and leave to stand.
2. Butter a cake dish measuring 20cm/8 inches in diameter and 5cm/2 inches deep. Line the base with a circle of non-stick baking paper.
3. Break the eggs into a bowl and beat lightly with a fork. Sift the flour with the baking powder and mixed spice. Peel and core the apples and chop the flesh finely.
4. Beat the butter with the sugar until light and fluffy. Gradually beat in the eggs. Add the flour mixture, apples, saffron mixture and milk or apple juice and fold in.
5. Spoon the mixture into the prepared dish and level the top, making a slight well in the centre.
6. Cook (do not cover) on Medium-High for 10–12 minutes or until the cake is just cooked at its centre and still slightly moist on the surface (a wooden cocktail stick inserted in the centre should come out clean).
7. Leave the cake to stand in its dish for 5 minutes before carefully running a knife round the sides and turning it out onto a cooling rack, removing the lining paper as you do so. Leave to cool.
8. Just before serving, sift a little icing sugar over the top.

Blueberry Shortcake

Try replacing the blueberries with other soft fruit, such as raspberries. Can be served warm as a dessert with cream.

Serves 8–10

150g/5½ oz butter, plus extra for greasing
1 small orange
200g/7 oz plain wholemeal flour
3 tbsp semolina
75g/2¾ oz soft light brown sugar
200g/7 oz fresh blueberries
Icing sugar, for dusting

1. Lightly butter the base of an ovenproof cake dish, 20cm/8 inches in diameter and 5cm/2 inches deep, and insert a circle of non-stick baking paper. Finely grate the rind from the orange.

2. Put the flour, orange rind and semolina into a mixing bowl. Cut the butter into small pieces and add to the flour. Using fingertips, rub the butter into the flour until the mixture resembles fine breadcrumbs. Stir in the brown sugar.

3. Spoon two-thirds of the mixture into the prepared dish, levelling the top and pressing down gently with the back of the spoon. Arrange the blueberries over the top. Scatter the remaining mixture evenly over the fruit – it need not cover the fruit completely.

4. Cook (do not cover) on Medium for about 10 minutes until just firm to the touch at the centre of the cake.

5. Leave to stand for 15 minutes before using a sharp knife to cut into wedges. Leave to cool completely before carefully lifting the wedges out of the dish, sifting over a little icing sugar and serving.

Coconut and Honey Drops

Dark brown sugar and honey give a dense chewy texture to these delicious little cakes. Perfect with a cup of tea or coffee. Double paper muffin cases are used in this recipe – to support the mixture during cooking – and the cakes are cooked in two batches.

Makes 12

55g/2 oz butter
125g/4½ oz soft brown sugar
1 tbsp clear honey
150g/5½ oz plain flour
1½ tsp ground mixed spice
55g/2 oz desiccated coconut
2 medium eggs
1 tbsp milk
Extra desiccated coconut, for sprinkling

1.   Put the butter, sugar and honey into a heatproof jug and cook (no need to cover) on High for 30–45 seconds, stirring once until the butter has melted. Stir well to dissolve the sugar. Leave to stand for 1 minute to cool.

2.   Into a mixing bowl, sift the flour and ground mixed spice, then stir in the coconut. Break the eggs into a small bowl, beat with a fork and stir them and the milk into the cooled butter mixture. Pour into the flour mixture and beat until thoroughly mixed. Spoon the mixture into twelve double muffin cases.

3.   Arrange six cakes around the edge of a large shallow dish or plate, leaving a small space between each one. Cook (do not cover) on High for 1½ minutes or until just cooked in the centre and still slightly moist on the surface (a wooden cocktail stick inserted in the centre should come out clean).

4.   Lift onto a cooling rack and immediately sprinkle a little coconut over the top of each one (the coconut will stick to the surface). Leave to cool.

5.   Cook the remaining six cakes, following steps 3 and 4.

6.   Remove the cake cases just before serving.

Raspberry and Apricot Jam

Lovers of all things sweet and sticky will enjoy this. The jam is made with frozen raspberries (though you could use fresh) and dried apricots (organic ones give the best flavour) to provide a taste of summer all year round. Make sure you use a very large bowl – the mixture is likely to boil up – and one that can withstand the high temperatures of boiling sugar. It is important not to cover the dish after the sugar has been added.

Makes about 900g/2 lb

150g/5½ oz organic dried apricots
300g/10½ oz frozen raspberries
2 tbsp fresh lemon juice
450g/1 lb granulated sugar, preferably golden variety

1. Finely chop the dried apricots and put into a large bowl with 150ml/¼ pint water. Cover and cook on High for 5 minutes.

2. Stir in the frozen raspberries and lemon juice. Cover and cook on High for 3–5 minutes until the fruit is very soft.

3. Add the sugar and stir until dissolved. Cook (do not cover) on High for about 5 minutes until the mixture comes to the boil.

4. Stir and then cook on Medium–High (do not cover) for about 10 minutes or until setting point is reached – test by putting a small spoonful onto a cold saucer: if a skin forms, it is ready to set; if not, continue cooking for a little longer.

5. With oven gloves, carefully remove the bowl from the microwave oven and set it on a heatproof surface. Leave to stand for 5 minutes then pour into warmed, sterilised jars and seal.

Apple Butter

Be sure to use a cooking container that can withstand a high temperature. Pass the fruit through a nylon sieve – a metal one may taint the flavour of the butter. A spoonful of calvados or brandy could be stirred in at the end of step 4.

Makes about 500g/1 lb 2 oz

900g/2 lb cooking apples, such as Bramley
125g/4½ oz soft light brown sugar
1 tsp ground cinnamon
Large pinch of ground cloves

1. Chop the apples (skin, cores and all) into small pieces.

2. Put all the ingredients into a casserole, cover and cook on High for 15–20 minutes, stirring occasionally, until the fruit is very soft.

3. Tip the mixture into a nylon sieve and use a wooden spoon to push the purée through into a clean casserole (you will probably need to do this in batches). Discard the mixture of skins and seeds remaining in the sieve.

4. Cook (do not cover) the apple purée on High for about 10–15 minutes, stirring once or twice, until the mixture is very thick and paste-like.

5. Spoon into warmed, sterilised jars and seal.

Lemon and Lime Curd

Home-made curd has a fabulous flavour. Spread on toast, add a spoonful to hot sweet pancakes or use as a filling for sponge cakes.

Makes about 450g/1 lb

1 large lemon
2 limes
3 medium eggs
125g/4½ oz unsalted butter
225g/8 oz caster sugar

1. Finely grate the rinds from the lemon and the limes. Cut each fruit in half and squeeze out the juice. Break the eggs into a bowl and beat with a fork until well mixed.

2. Cut the butter into small cubes and put into a large bowl. Add the sugar, juices and rinds.

3. Cook on High (do not cover) for 4 minutes, stirring once or twice, until the sugar has dissolved. Leave to cool for 5 minutes.

4. Stir a spoonful of the butter mixture into the beaten eggs then whisk into the hot butter mixture. Cook on Medium for 3–4 minutes, stirring every minute until the curd thickens.

5. Pour into warmed, sterilised jars and seal.

Seville Orange and Grapefruit Marmalade

Tangy marmalade is traditionally eaten at breakfast, but it is also good spooned onto crumpets or served with hot or cold hams, or pork. Seville oranges are only available in January and give a lovely sharp taste, but you can use ordinary oranges.

Makes about 450g/1 lb

1 grapefruit
2 Seville oranges
1 tbsp lemon juice
350g/12 oz preserving sugar

1. Put the kettle on to boil. Thinly peel the grapefruit and oranges to remove the rind only, with no white pith attached. Cut the rinds into thin shreds. Halve the fruits and squeeze out the juices, reserving the pips. Cut up the remaining flesh (the fruit shells) into small pieces and put them with the pips onto a square of muslin. Pull up the corners and tie them together securely.

2. Pour the three fruit juices into a large bowl, add the muslin bag and 150ml/¼ pint boiling water (from the kettle) and leave to stand for 1 hour.

3. Add an extra 150ml/¼ pint boiling water (from the kettle). Cover and cook on High for about 20 minutes or until the peel is very tender.

4. Stir in the sugar. Cook (do not cover) on High for about 5 minutes, stirring every minute, until the sugar has dissolved.

5. Once the sugar has dissolved, cook (do not cover) on High for about 15 minutes or until the marmalade reaches setting point – test by putting a small spoonful onto a cold saucer: if a skin forms, it is ready to set; if not, continue cooking for a little longer.

6. Lift out, drain and discard the muslin bag. Leave the marmalade to stand on a heatproof surface for 10–15 minutes before pouring into warmed, sterilised jars and sealing.

Apple and Walnut Chutney

Goes particularly well with most types of cheese. Try it also in sandwiches filled with ham, pork or chicken. Sometimes we add a good pinch of chilli powder to the mixture in step 2. Keep refrigerated and use within 2 months.

Makes about 450g/1 lb

300g/10½ oz onions
1 lemon
500g/1 lb 2 oz cooking apples, such as Bramley
50g/1¾ oz sultanas or raisins
150g/5½ oz demerara sugar
150ml/¼ pint malt vinegar
1 tsp ground mixed spice
½ tsp salt

1. Finely chop the onions. Finely grate the rind from the lemon and squeeze out the juice. Peel the apples, remove and discard their cores and chop the fruit into small pieces.

2. Put all the ingredients into a large bowl or casserole and mix well. Cover and cook on High for about 10 minutes or until the mixture comes to the boil.

3. Remove the cover and continue cooking on High for about 20 minutes, stirring occasionally, until the mixture is very thick and hardly any liquid remains.

4. Spoon into warm, sterilised jars and seal.

Index